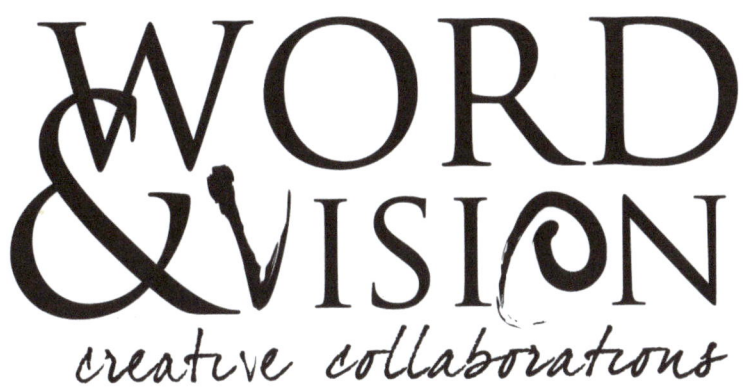

WORD &VISION
creative collaborations

VOLUME ONE

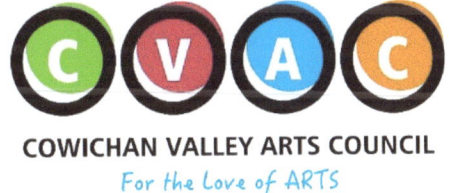

COWICHAN VALLEY ARTS COUNCIL

For the Love of ARTS

Word and Vision Creative Collaborations, Volume One

ISBN: 978-0-9948281-0-1

ACKNOWLEDGEMENTS

Word and Vision Committee

Pauline Thompson
Wendy Robison
Melanie Higgs
Alisha Baker
Brigette Furlonger
Judy Brayden
Gail Robertson
Maureen Shayler

Photography

Kerry Davis
Frank Wall
Brigette Furlonger
Judy Brayden

Photo editor and book interior

Gail Robertson

Book cover design

Alisha Baker

INTRODUCTION

Verse and Vision (now Word and Vision) has long been a favourite of members of the Cowichan Valley Arts Council (CVAC) and visitors to our art space, PORTALS. And why not? Writers' inspired poems and prose are transformed into visual feasts and interpretive performances, which delight and intrigue. Normally, art creation is a solitary pleasure. Opportunities like this to collaborate are rare and stimulating for artists, and a delightful change for readers and viewers.

Word and Vision Creative Collaborations, Volume One has been a labour of love for everyone involved. This compilation lets CVAC and the Word and Vision participants share with the world the written and visual treats that make this show so popular in the Cowichan Valley and beyond. We have also included photos of the performance artists and a description of their contributions.

*   *   *

THE CHALLENGE
BEHIND THE PROJECT

Collaboration can be a frightening thought for the individual who resides in each of our creative hearts. *However, is it not in art that the true nature of collaboration is revealed?* Participants who take that challenge thrust a ball into motion, to be caught or bounced in untold directions by their new partner(s). Together they share and rejoice, watching its path near and veer and even collide with them. It takes a rich and deep and telling course. Thanks to all who rose to that challenge and shared that journey together.

And now, please turn the page and enjoy . . . .

CONTENTS
POEMS/PROSE
COLLABORATIVE WORKS

A FLOCK OF ROBINS

A flock of robins
Drops down through snowberry brambles
Moving stealthily
In muted travelling clothes
Twittering wintry songs.

Laura Anderson

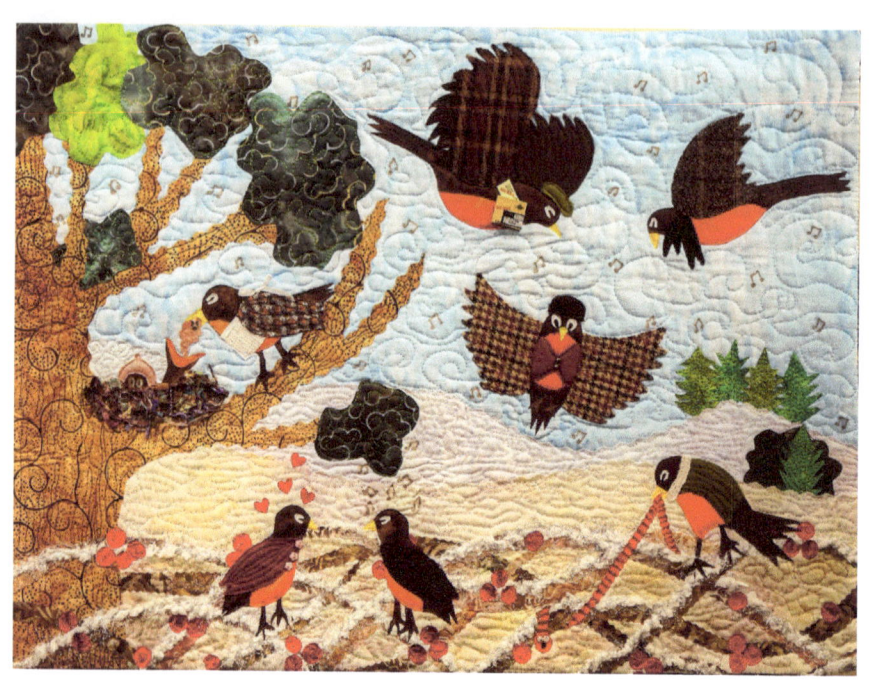

SPRING RETURNS
Elaine Hennecker

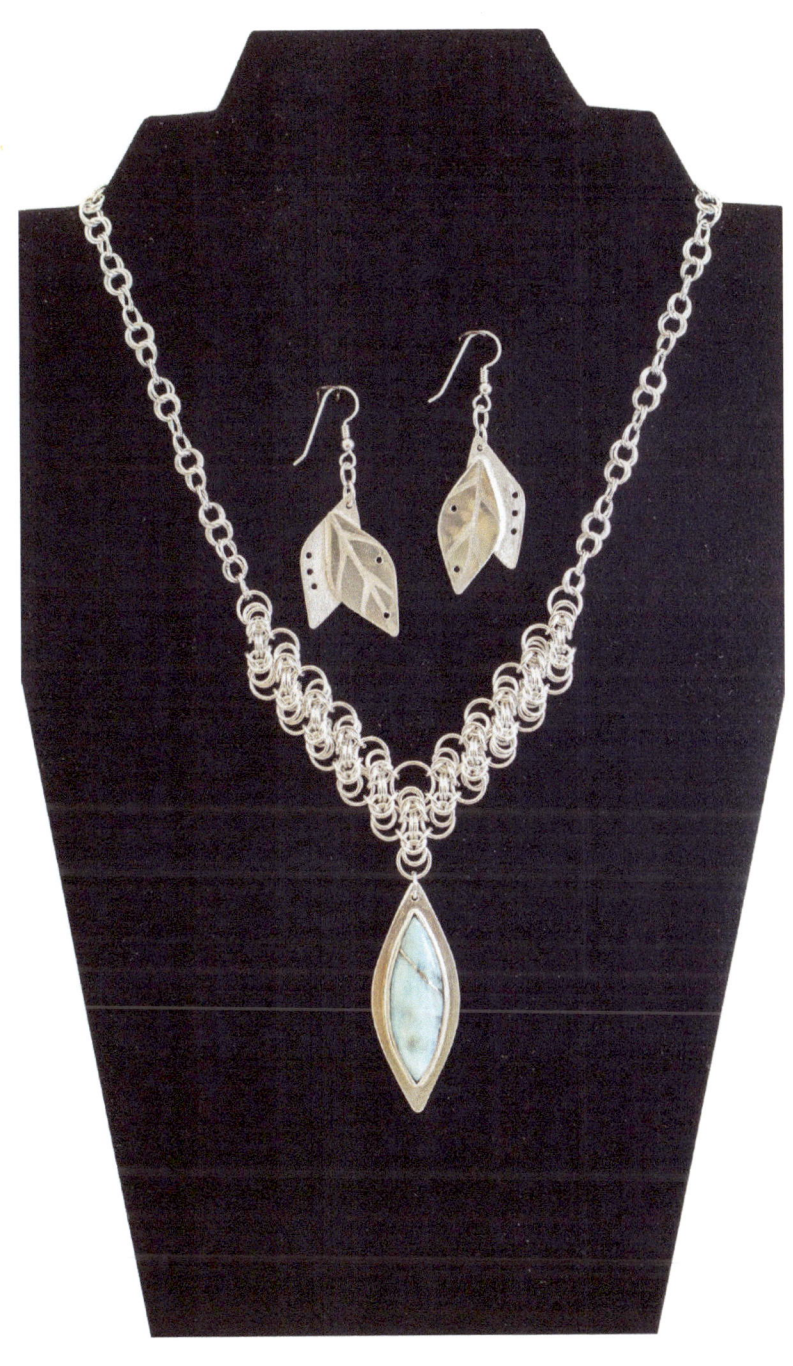

FLIGHT PATH
Karola Schabernak

SEPIA

These are the train tracks.
Lazy pebbles pinging on abandoned steel,
popsicle sticks tossed in the yellow grass.

This is the hot breeze.
The smell of asphalt and dust.
The nodding heads of plants turned to seed.

This is tanned skin and the lake.
The slanting rays of a late sun.
A rough-hewn surface, those sharp points of light.

This is the dew-stained night.
Beneath a flimsy blanket -
the way your feet rested on mine.

This well-worn path.
These memories that keep count in real time,
your fingertips on old shapes.

This is the uneasy pilgrimage.

To these hazy, distracted days.

To these nights that smell like the lake.

Jennifer Barnes Van Elk

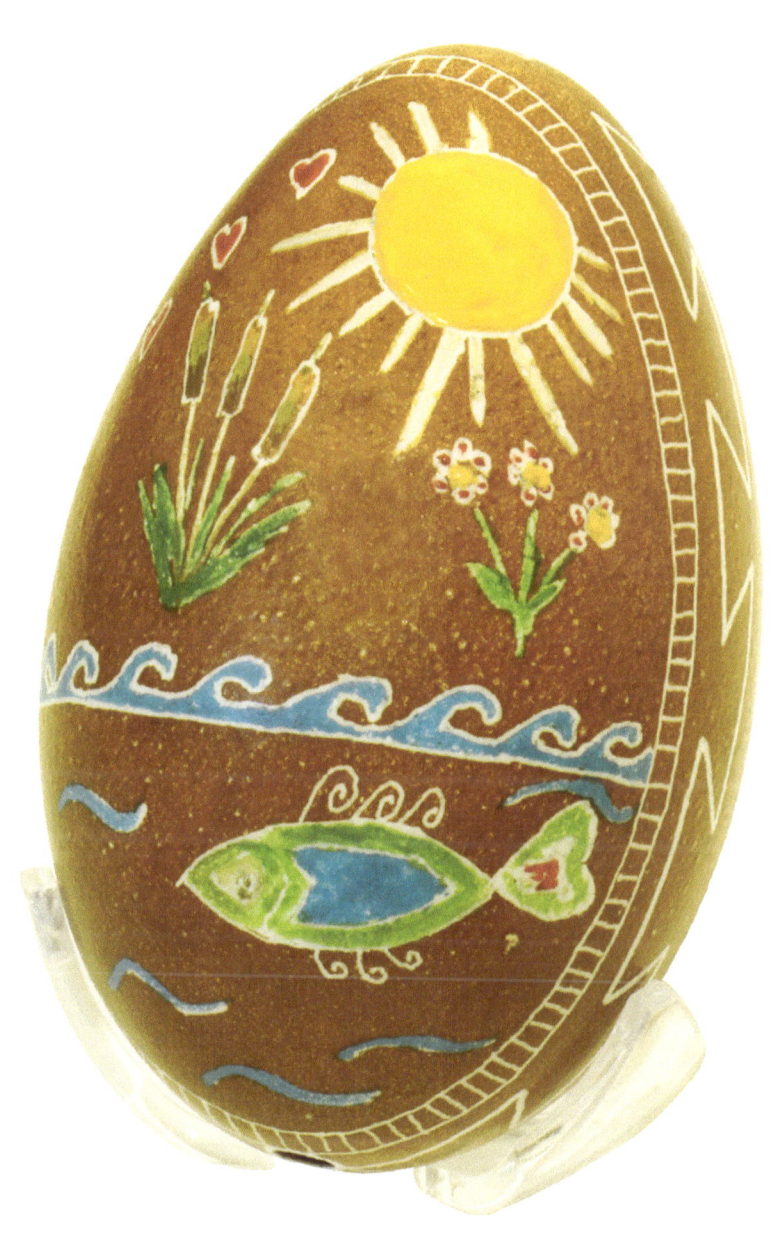

SEPIA
Pauline Thompson

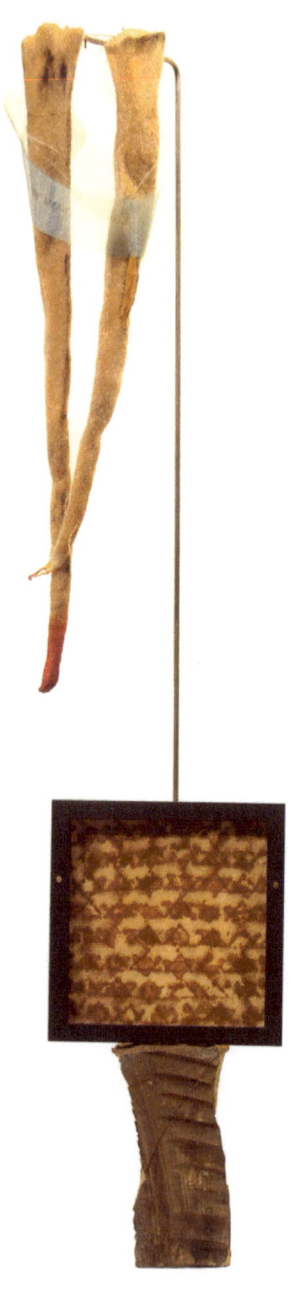

ANCESTRAL POEM
Joanne Circle

6

ONCE UPON A WINTER'S DREAMING

Take away the leaves and the underside of the forest rises
in splattered bark and blurry edges that move if not watched
as emptied branches dribble silver beads of rain and
black trees grow beards like tattered gauze on gaunt faces

Dream quest child-eyed into the thickening and you will see
a long antlered wolf head dangling between maples
a shaggy emu holding its breath on a fallen log and
a string of furry turtles winding their long necks up a wide tree

When a crinkly fingered long eyed treeman turns to listen and
the fattened leg of a giant woolly spider inches towards you
un-make believe and flee as thin boned maples bend over you and
a raven follows above, its gurgling croak like laughter in your ears

Debbie Bateman

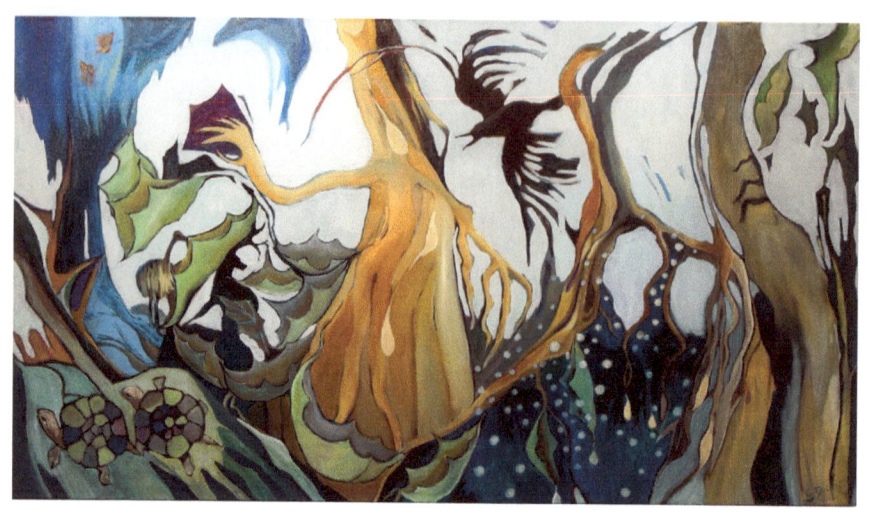

WINTER'S DREAMING
Shirley Dickie

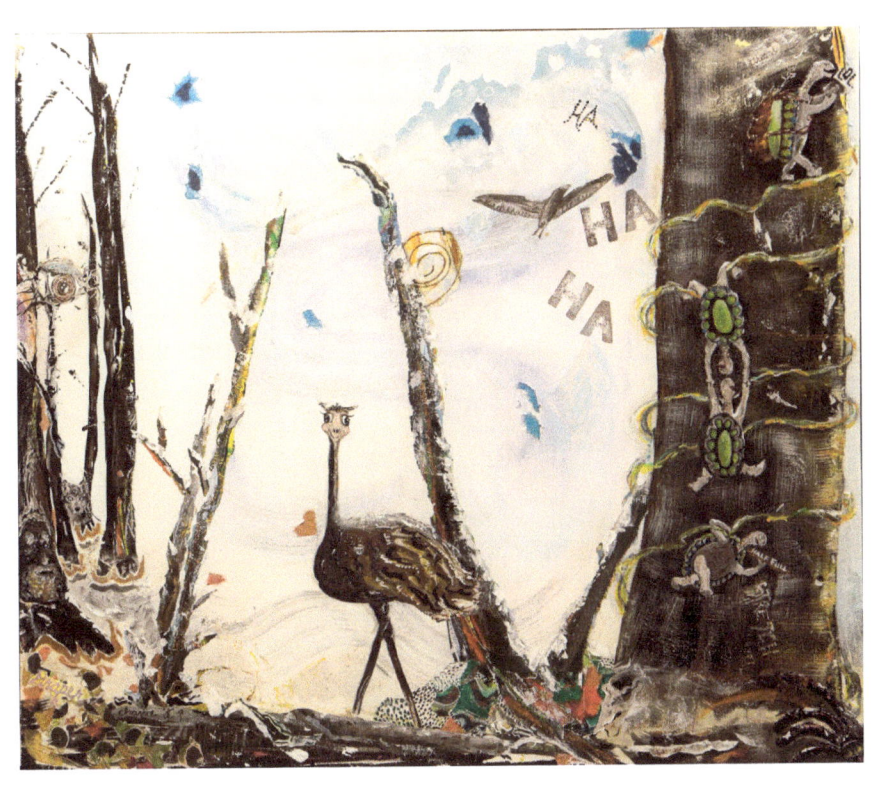

A WINTER'S DAYDREAM
Donna Draper

TRAVELLING

Traveling onward
quiet
looking out
soft mist
covers the flat land
everything low
houses, barns
stubby green trees
mix of white birches
flash their long legs out from between
green firs
tinge of yellow acknowledging
the coming of Autumn
Crows and Ravens
swoop overhead
seeking feast

Dogs are dog-tired
eyes shut
sitting up
nodding, head down,
then sleeping…

Margitta Ben-Oliel

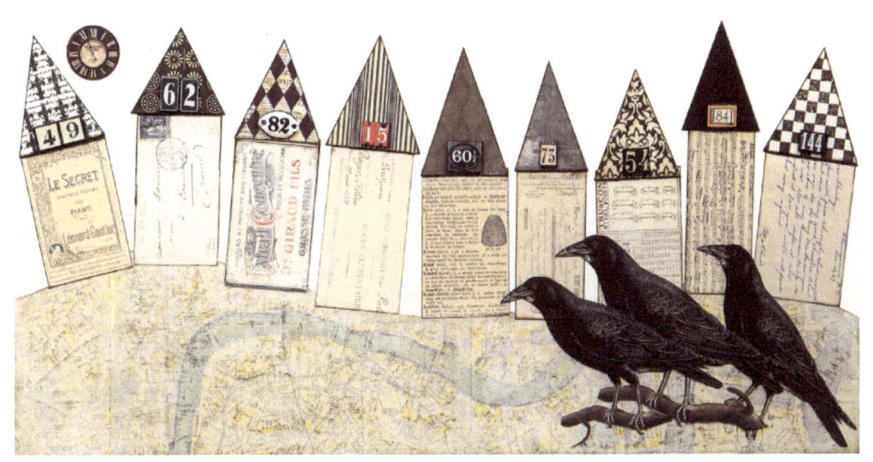

BLACKBIRDS
Wilma Millette

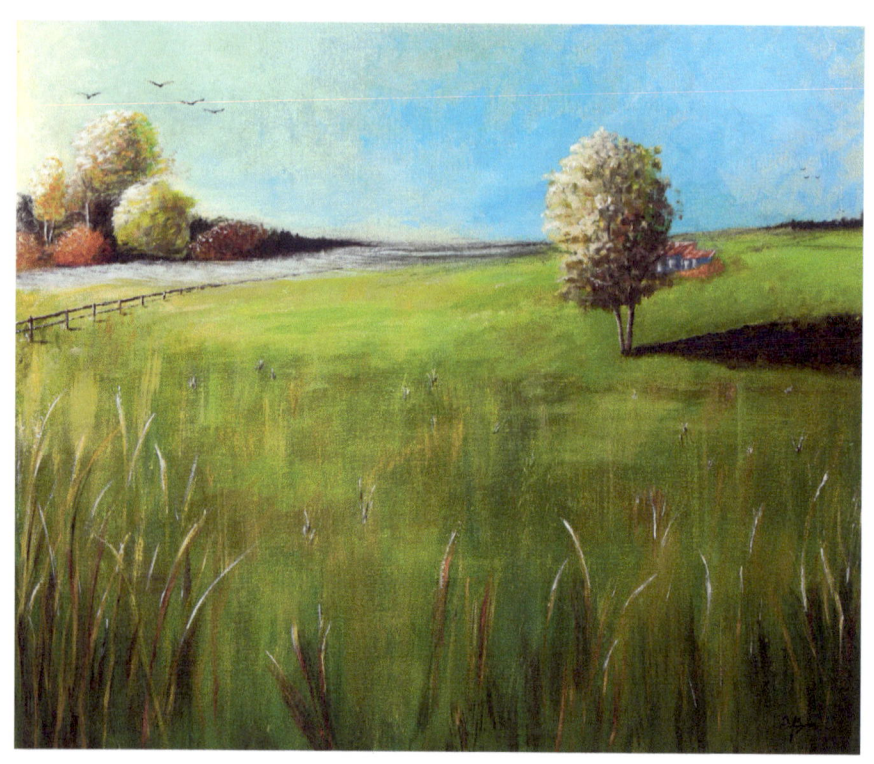

TRAVELLING
Erin Byron

THE OLD HOUSE

Across the field at the edge of a wood
    the old house stands alone.
It's empty now, and silently looks
    at a garden that's overgrown.
The paint has peeled from window and door,
    the shutters have fallen away,
And lie askew on unkempt ground
    in jumbled disarray.
The tiles on the roof are covered with moss,
    the windows are dusty and cracked.
The old oak door is splintered and scratched,
    and the gutters with leaves are tight-packed.
The un-pruned branches of the trees
    spread arms against the sky,
And offer welcome solitude
    to birds that fly on high.
By the broken down fence a fork sadly leans,
    its tines all twisted and bent
From digging up root crops each year
    in the Fall, a happy and joyous event.
The pear tree that used to be loaded with fruit
    does not yield its abundance today.
The swing where the children spent laughter-filled hours
    hangs abandoned, with no-one to play.
Leaving the shade of the sheltering wood
    the deer come to nibble the flowers.
They walk through the garden with beauty and grace,
    and while away many sweet hours.
There are rabbits that scamper, and frolic, and munch,
    then dance in the morn's early light.
While the wily raccoons with their babies in tow
    play under cover of night.
The owls hoot their solitary calls 'neath the moon,
    while the crows "caw" to welcome the morn.
The sweet gentle sound of the two mourning doves
    gives way to the song-birds at dawn.

Dragonflies, butterflies, insects and mice
    fly and scurry around their domain.
Each with their own special purpose in life
    and a link in the life-giving chain.
What of the people who lived in the house,
    their laughter, their joy and their tears?
You can still feel their spirits, and capture the love,
    that somehow lives on through the years.
For the whispers and echoes that speak of the past
    remind us of days left behind.
And we look to the future with promise and hope
    as we search for new treasures to find.

Christine Bennett

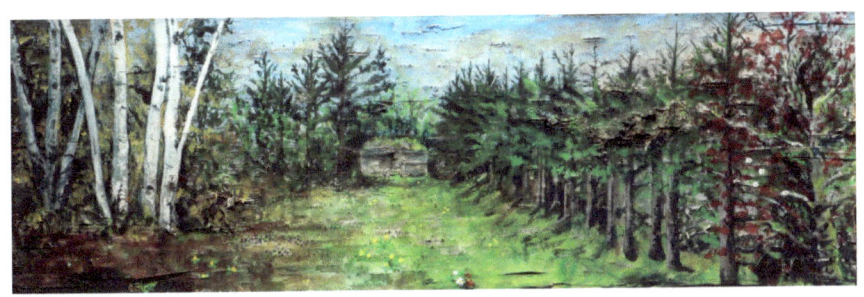

UNTITLED
Kassandra Simon

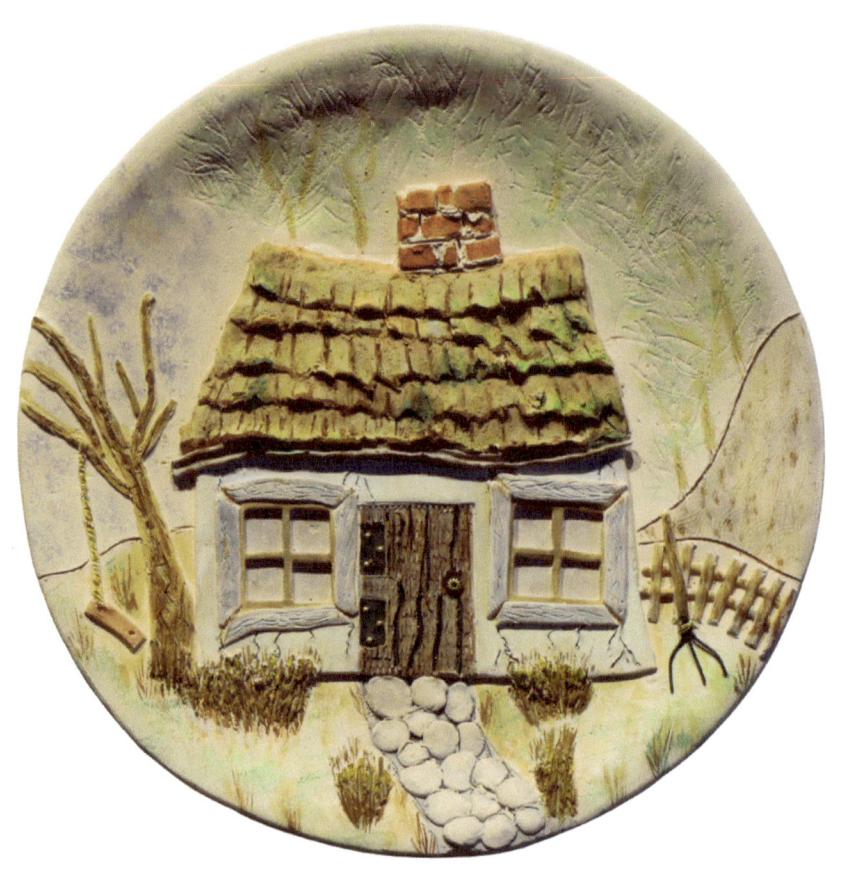

THE OLD HOUSE
Penny Jones

FEMINESSENCE (A GODDESS PRAYER)

My womb is bathed in golden light
Tiny stars swirling inside
Twinkling, laughing in the void
Peace, tranquility flowing through my body
Like mother's milk

Ecstasy engorging my breasts
Nipples straining
For release, for touch
For light, for love
Body arched to give and to receive
The miracles of spirit
Born into flesh

My woman's spirit in many guises
Soft, yielding
Hard, uncompromising
Seeker of Truth
Breast of Hope
Body of Life Eternal

Alara Bretanne

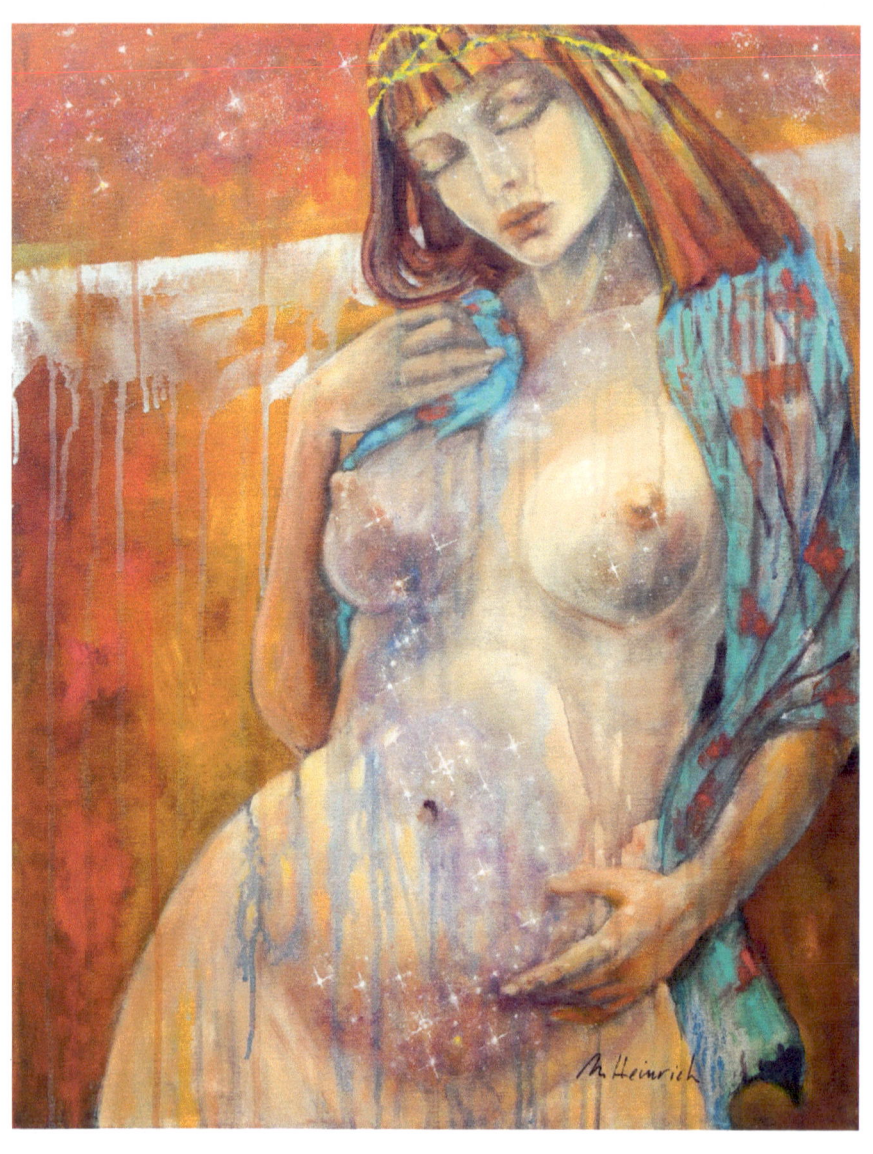

FEMINESSENCE – A GODDESS PRAYER
Michael Heinrich

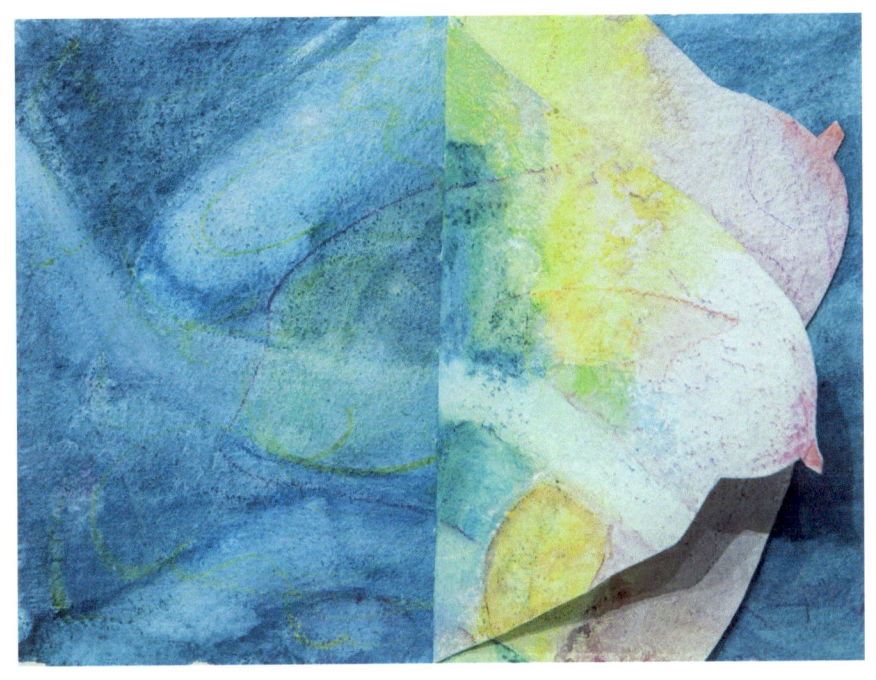

PLEASE HANDLE WITH CARE
Melanie Circle

MANNING PARK FULL MOON

The moon caresses the virgin snow.
Fir trees rise like sentinels about her.
The snaking river brushes her naked flanks,
shudders, and moves on.
It is not time to take her yet.
She feels his touch
and knows her destiny

Mari Brown

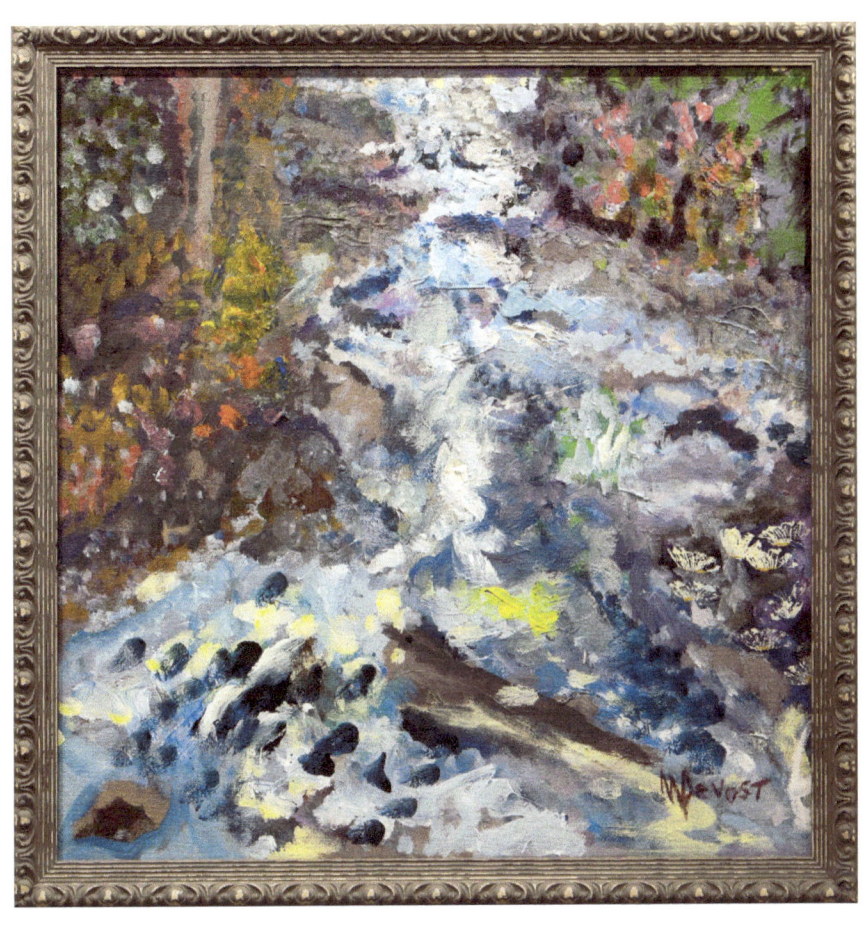

SUZANNA
Michele Devost

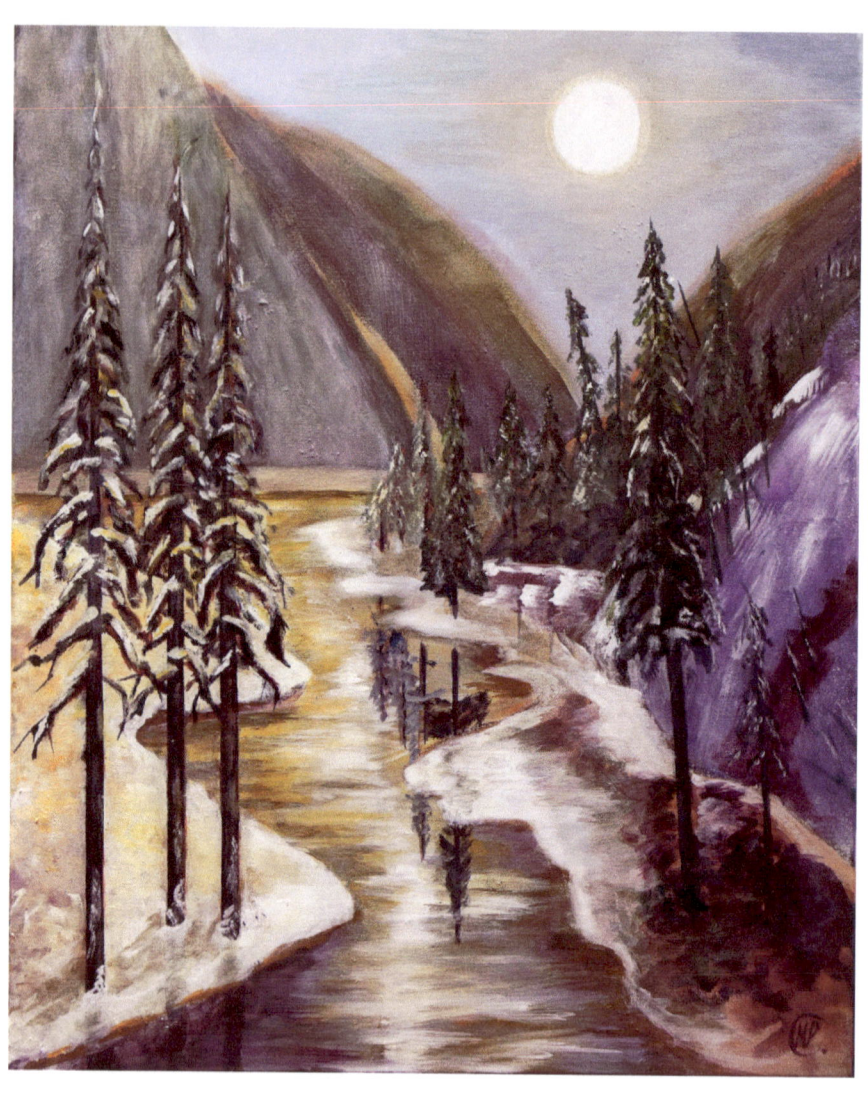

MOONLIGHT IN MANNING PARK
Tricia Cadorette

THE EYES
The Prologue

He awoke. Heart thumping. Its eyes held him in a state of rigor. Frozen terror. Red eyes. Glowing from within. If only he could break contact, then he could run for it.

His stomach roiled with clenching fear as the creature grew – morphing sharply – not a humongous rat at all! A dirty grey, sharp featured face framed by scruffy matted mousy coloured hair. Dressed in.... No! It couldn't be! No! The horror of it!

Realization hit, slamming him back to consciousness. Too freaked by the vision to even be aware of the acid tears leaking to his pillow, he scrubbed his scarred hands over his eyes. Recognition brought despair – filling him, but calming him into release from the nightmare.

It was him. But it wasn't him. Not anymore. It was a twisted vision, a macabre vision of those days of utter desperation. Now he connected to it. Driving through the slums today and stopping the car.... The feel of the place. Abandonment. The fear was that of a six year old dropped into the hell of vying with sewer rats for the right to search the garbage in back of the cafe. The desperation of hunger driving him.

Learning the meaning of bravery.

The eyes had been his. The eyes of a cornered rat. The eyes of a survivor.

Susan Christensen

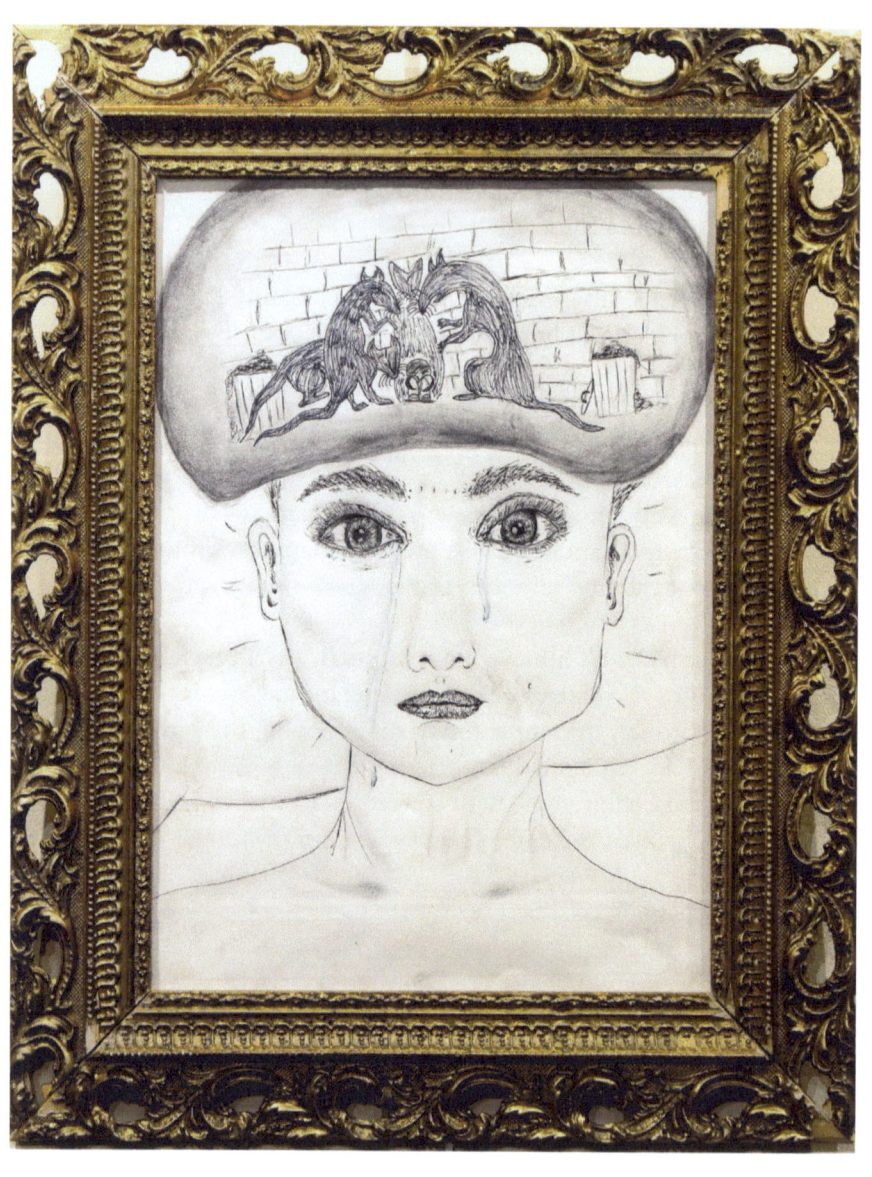

THE EYES
Emma Kononowicz

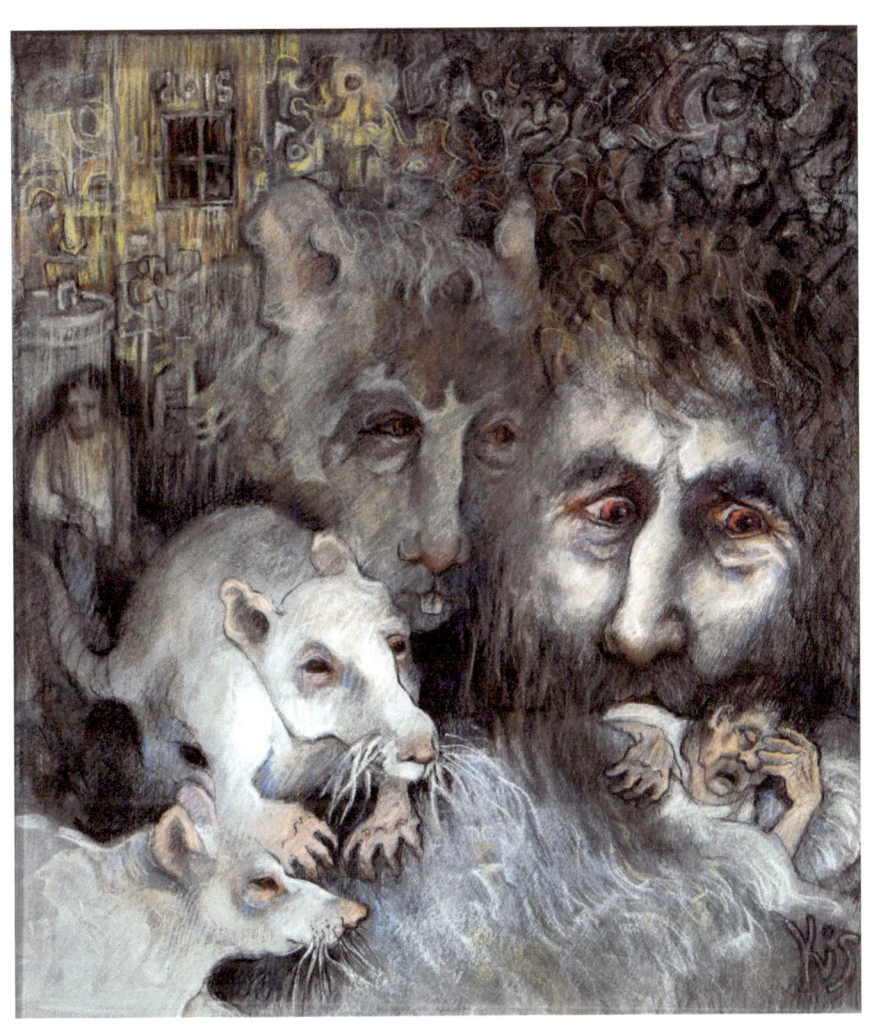

THE EYES
Kaye Smille

CHAT

A chat room shimmering dark
Until she types "hi"
And he writes "hi there" back
A conversation starts
His words on the left
Hers on the right
A bubble throbs
Indicating new entries
Single lines of phrases
Black on white shine bright
Pulling tenuous strings
Of each other's heart
Lines come faster
Some from the left
Others the right
Entwining fingers of words
To each other's delight
Binding them together
With stolen moments night after night
Days turn to weeks
Now, after weeks have turned to months
He starts to tease
She can't stop her flirt
It grows with ease
Even blossoms when he queries
The panties beneath her skirt
Safety within the miles
Of internet cable links
Until one of them says:
"It's time to meet don't you think?"

Brigette Furlonger

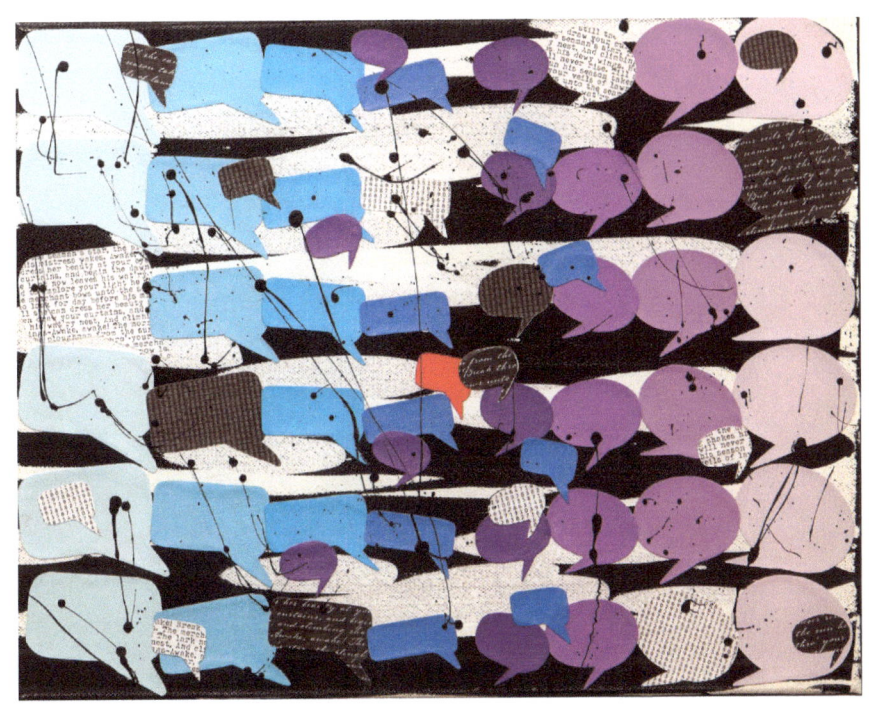

CHAT
Angela Cannon

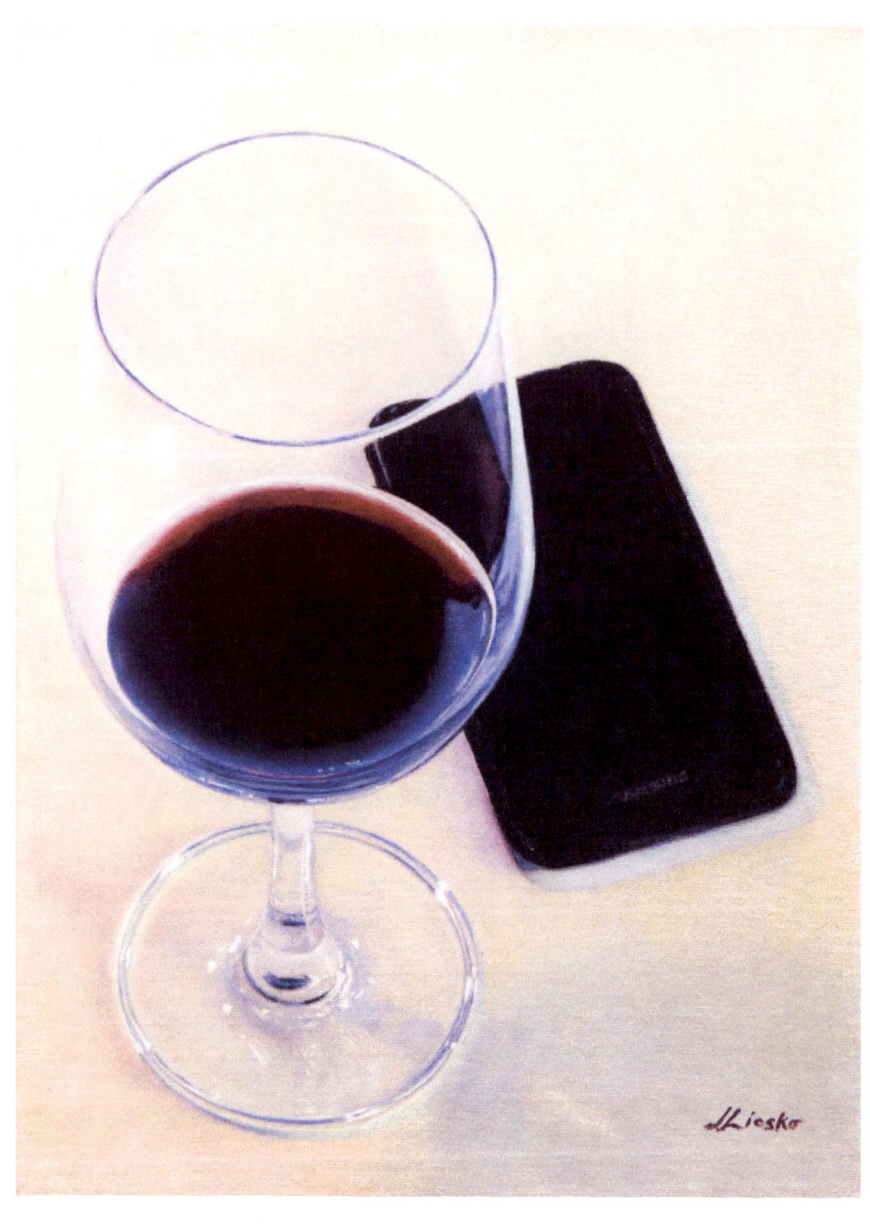

THE CALL
Joanne Licsko

SISTERS

When love was less than,
When life was sand that slipped,
When tears dripped down the cheek
Of the small girl that I was
You were there.

We shared mumps and bumps
And held hands to climb stairs
To a dark place with no space to breath.
The sun would bleed through cracks in the walls.

When halls where long and narrowing
You would hold me and sing.
And I was transported
To the minarets of Spain;
The Winter Palace of the Czars
Where I could be anything
I could dream.

The space between now and then;
There and here
Began in the stories you would read.
You introduced me
To the charm that twists and sparkles,
The strand of love on which I dance,
You holding one end and my paramour
The other.

Sandra Goth

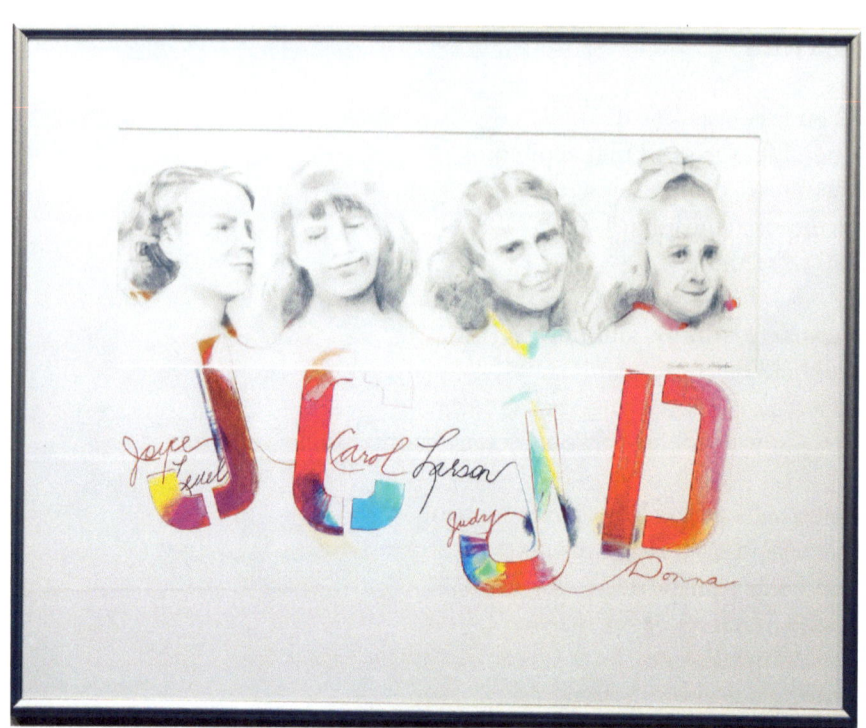

SISTERS
Judy Brayden

STORM

The stars are bright, yes, so bright,
And yet the wind is louder, booming inside,
The trees sway left, then right,
And skewer my heart, like a branch in the wind.

The thunder, the lightning,
The bang, the flash,
Brighter than anything I've ever seen.

The wind is pushing feverishly against my windows,
And the doors rattle in response,
I can feel the movement,
The rolling thunder and the impending rain.

But yet the stars are still bright, yes, so bright,
And there might still be hope for us yet.

Jacqueline Groicher

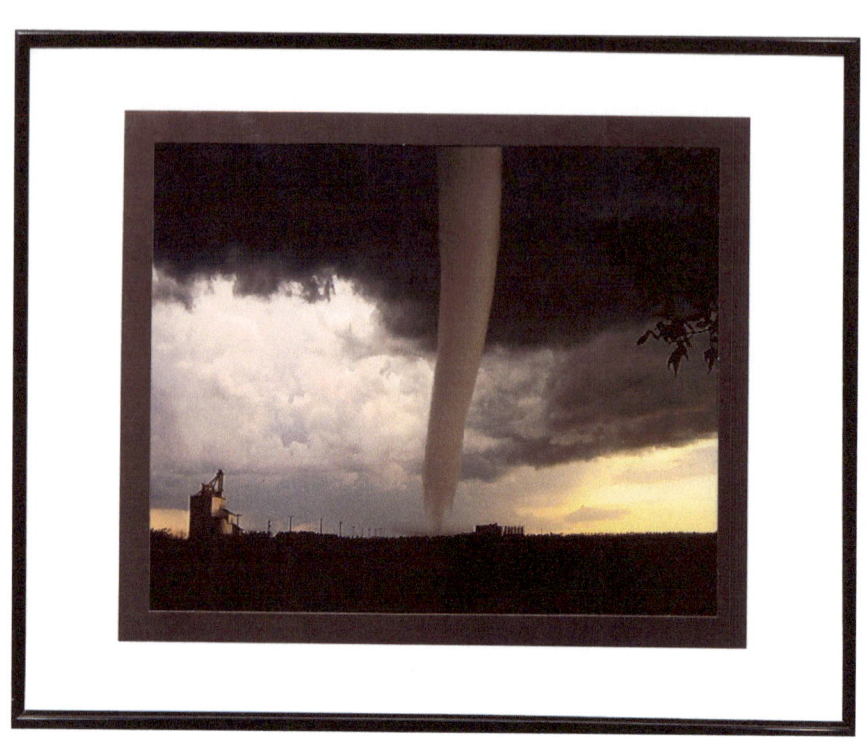

THE STORM
Robert Parkinson

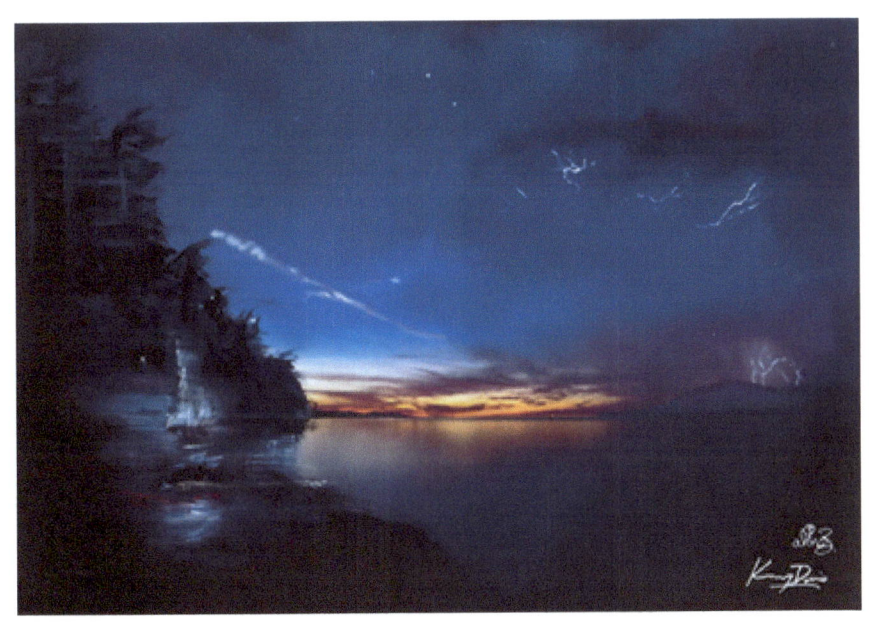

REFLECTIONS ON THE STORM
Kerry Davis and Alisha Baker

MY PEACH SOPHIA
A 'Medieval' Love Song

No maid however young and fair,
Or blue her eye or gold her hair,
Or soft her blush or light her step
Can ever hope to compare
With the charms of my Sofia.

Faithful and trusting is my love,
In all her deeds the peaceful dove.
With sweet kisses and caress
From me all pain she doth remove
With hand and heart, my dear Sofia.

And now I do both swear and tell
To you, who knows and loves me well:
Trust that when my word I give,
None can stop me, not even hell,
Nor keep me from my precious love, Sofia.

I vow to be faithful and true,
To shield and always comfort you.
I would die before I fail
In all ways to love and honor you,
My darling peach, Sofia.

Rebecca Hazell

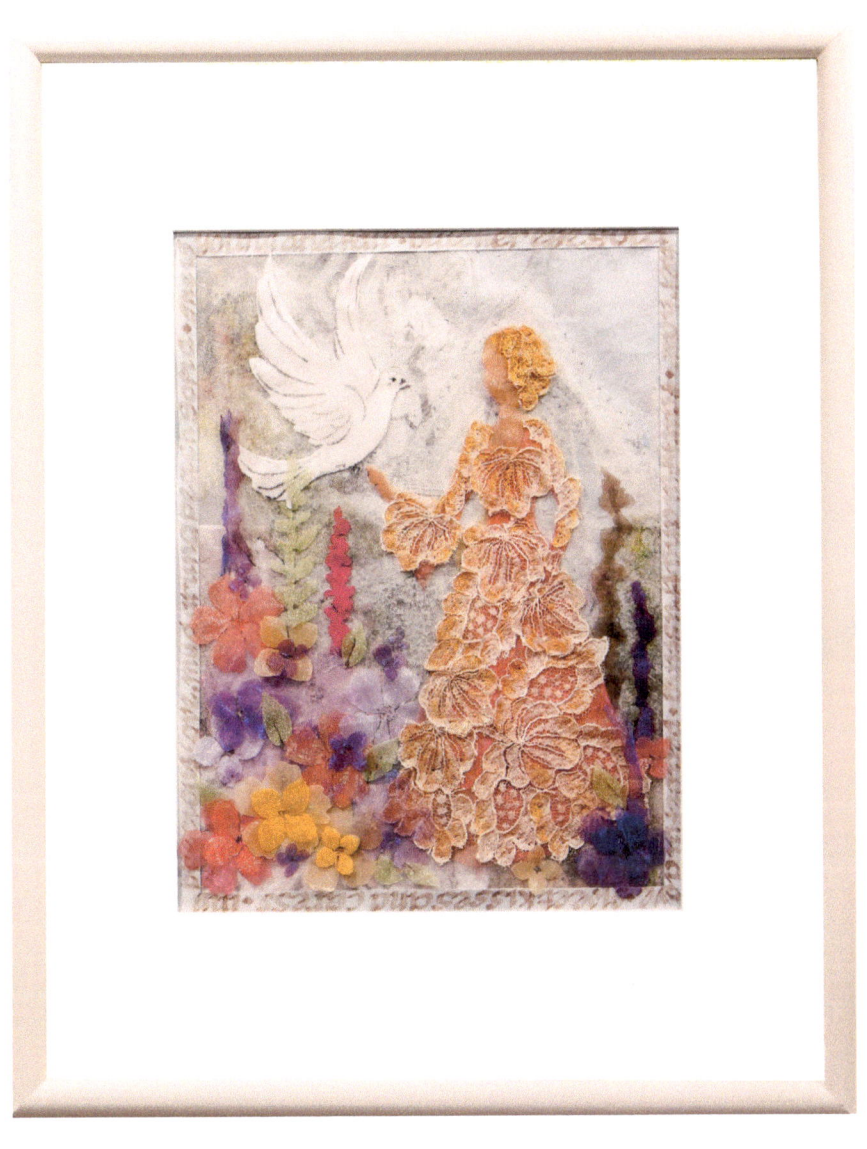

MY PEACH SOPHIA
Gill Riordan

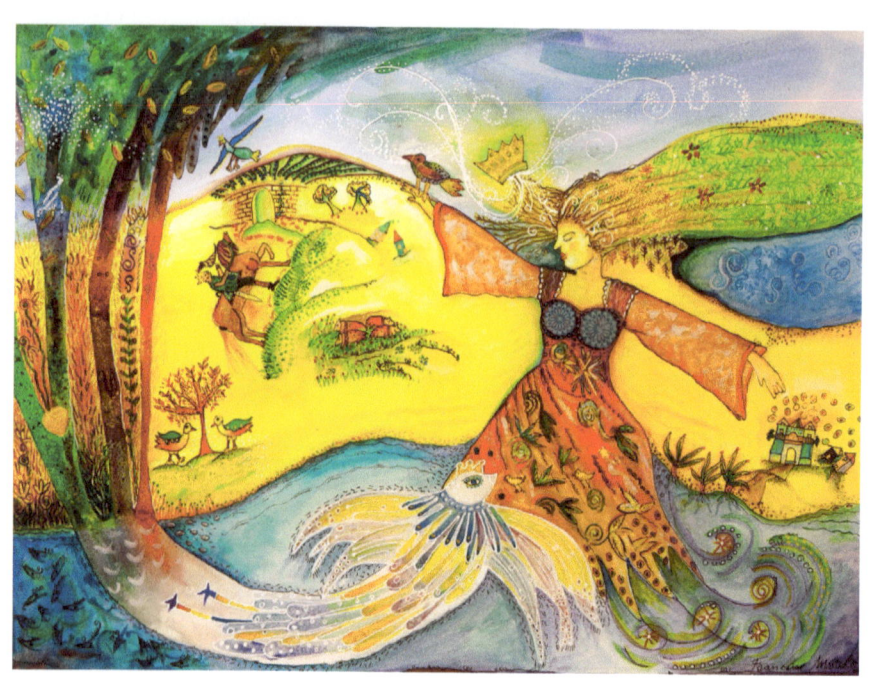

MY PEACH SOPHIA·
Françoise Moulin

THE GREEN MAN

In mid-winter, the Green Man dreams,
bark-bound, oak round, he sweats dark tannin,
breathes a musty thrumming through trunk and branch;
bulges a gnarly codpiece.

He dreams of the fruits of green,
tomatoes swelling under modest, inadequate leaves,
ripenings of deep, unembarrassed red.
And the pendulous, blushing haunch of pears,
smarting from the hungry wasp.
He can't help himself, roots through frosty earth
to finger the sleeping bulbs.

Who heeds his solitary oak in snowy field?
Delicate tracery on polished, pewter sky
where hides his crucible of fire,
his tinderbox heart beating with the icy crackle of light?

We do not see the tiny agitations,
the shivering synapse of his private ecstasy
forging energy from freezing air
with great bellows of green.

But wait instead, until his leer appears,
spewing leaves among the ivy, to offer thanks—
plant naked words on fallow page
cast notes across the silence
shape nothing into something—
and revive our hopes with dreams of green.

Melanie Higgs

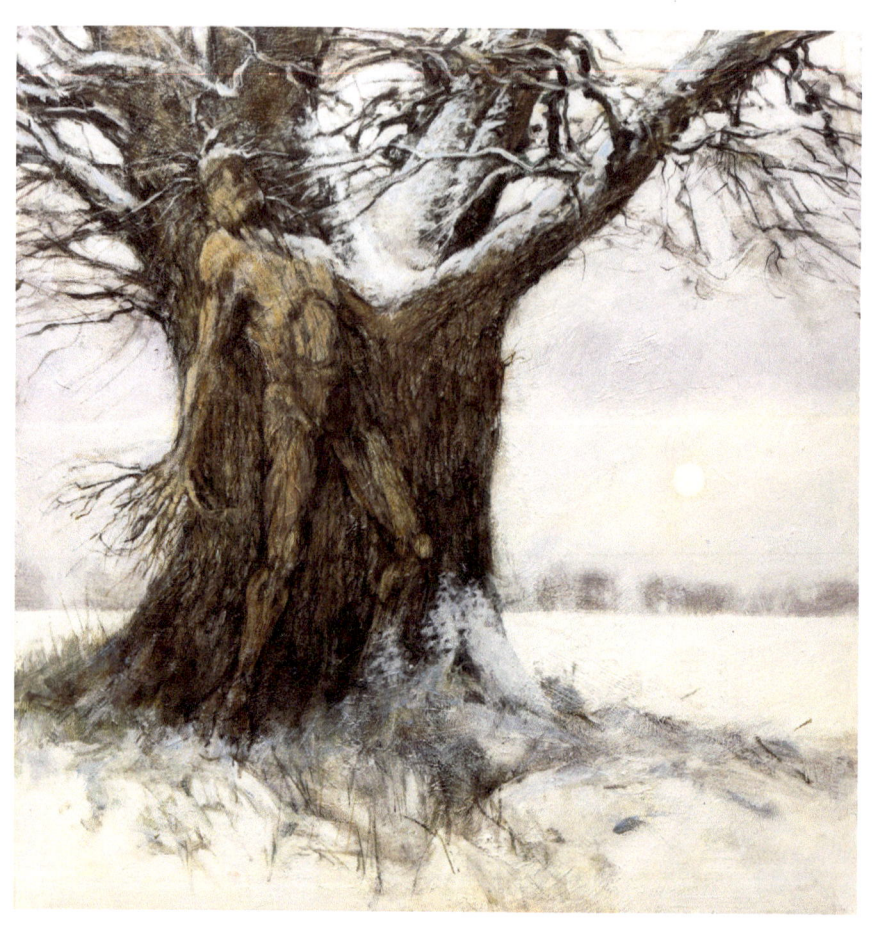

THE GREEN MAN
Sharron Campbell

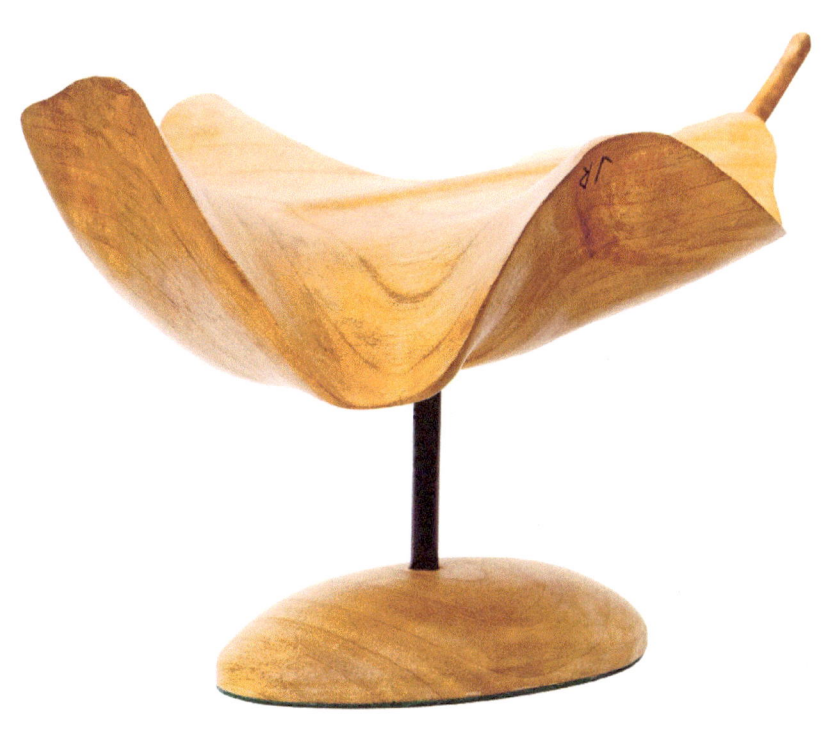

CANCION A LA JACARANDA
Jeff Ratcliff

ONLY SHADES OF GREEN

The view of Mt. Tolmie was slightly out of focus. A bit of fog she thought, or maybe just urban smoke. Wood burning fires, raked leaves piled, their last smoldering gasps releasing thin white vertical columns. Below her at a steep angle lay the lawn, cut close for winter. Rhododendrons, ferns, spreading junipers were easily spotted, growing in the encirclement around the grass. What were the others – those silver green, yellow green, blue green – thin spikes, flat leaves, wild branches, clipped limbs? No rose bushes here, she thought. No droopy daisies, or hydrangeas turning purple – remains of bright blooms of summer, but for one chrysanthemum. Even so, its golden brown flowers were about to go. A deer stood boldly confident. Bending to her supper, the garden lost its last bit of colour. Green she thought, just green.

Beverly Koski

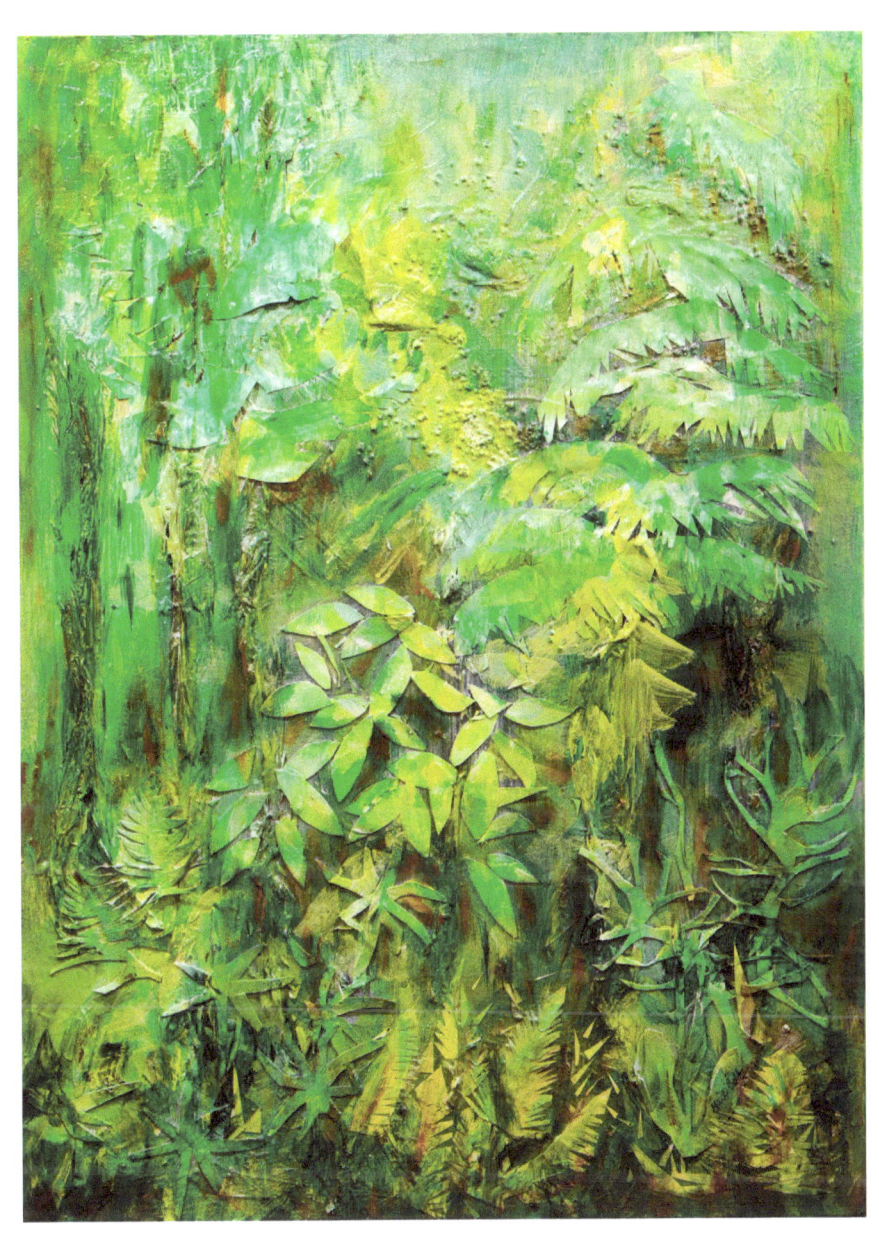

JUST GREEN
Gail Robb

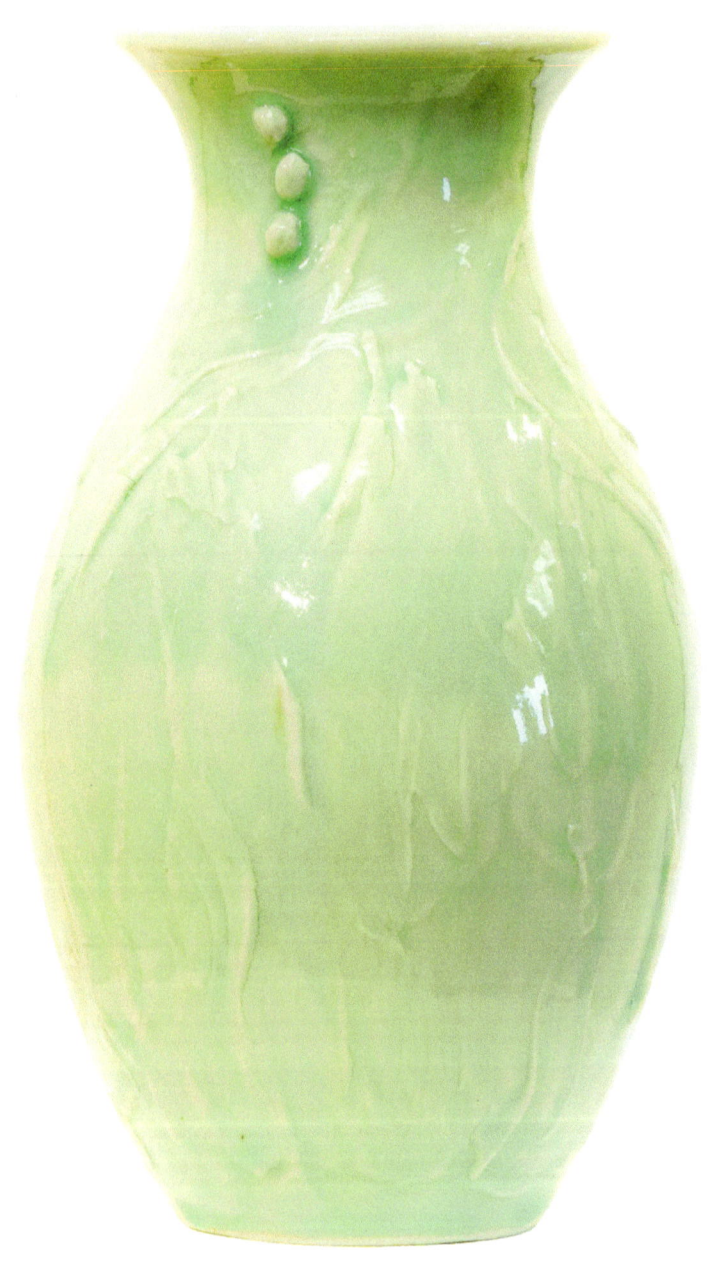

SHADES OF GREEN
Jane Wolters

DAISY PETAL DREAM

It is a Daisy Petal Dream
He loves me, she loves me not
Early morning meadow
Alive with dew clad webs
Glistening and sparkling
With rainbow hue
In the soft morning breeze
Beckoning imagination
Emotions without frame
What name have I
Amidst such as this

I am the Daisy and the Dew
And the web
My heart resonates
With sweet yearning
Swelling my breast
I am home
Not in words
But as foam
Upon a boundless sea
With divine understanding
Just Being

Words can only touch
What can not be explained
This is all I have to offer
Tis a Daisy Petal Dream

Paul Manuel

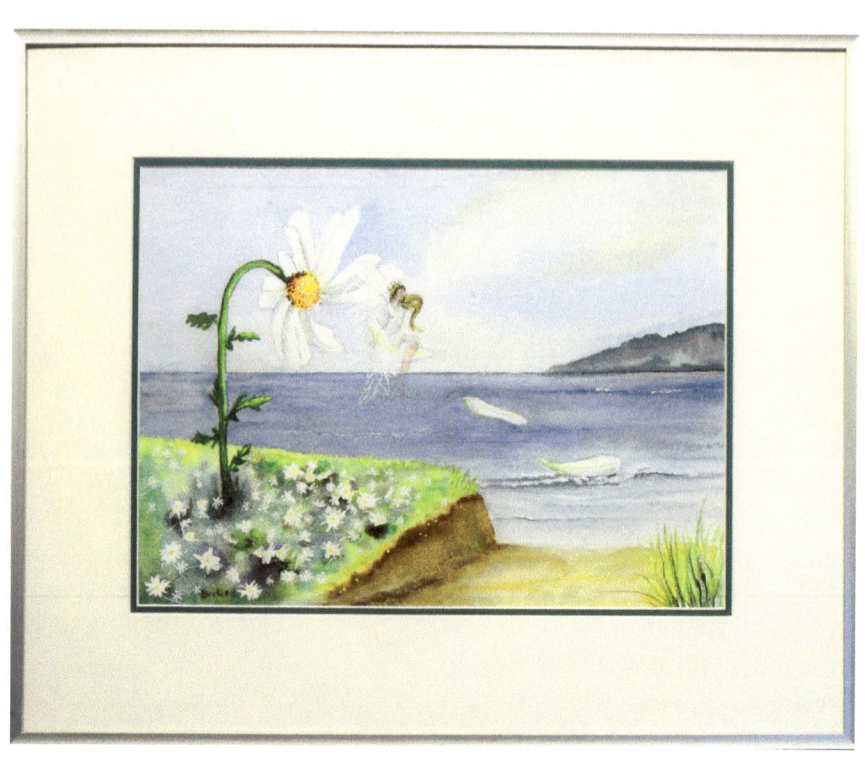

DAISY PETAL
Beckie Hutchinson

WHEN I'M OLD AND LONELY

Ahh, what a breathtaking sight to behold!
It's sunset time, the colours are warm and bold!
I could kiss the sky the maker of the heaven's has for me painted.
Like a gentle lover that wraps her love with arms soft and tender,
The darkness is slowly enveloping and kissing the town of Mill Bay,
Nestling by the shores of the salmon bearing Pacific Ocean.
The birds of prey fish their days away hovering over this rocky beach,
Like they have done since the beginning of time.
I weep not for what once was, which is no more.
Yet to the core, in a way, I am tickled more and more
Longing for what could have been.
With a soul that is bruised and broken like an open minefield,
As if I had no one to hold tight but myself through the night.
How so I take time to pick at thy reflection in the salt waters.
The fine lines and wrinkles startle me not, for it is the mark of the
    seasons.
And for what never was mine, I shall not cry,
But cherish the beauty that each season forth brings.
Polishing my rugged and jagged, sweet, cute face, or at least I tell my
    self so!
Watching all that pass me by as if I was invisible,
All while this fiery fire burns inside of me.
Longing for someone to kiss these wrinkles of mine.
Older I have grown, but love has not ebbed from my soul one bit.
Love I still vigorously do as you in your prime years.
The orgasms are profound and spiritual now that they are spaced.
Time does not wait for you and me.
The sea rises, the sea falls. The moon waxes the moon wanes.
I pray that it will be soon that the crickets sing again in my repose.
Till the end of time, to the moon and back, I will always love you!

Tafadzwa Matamba

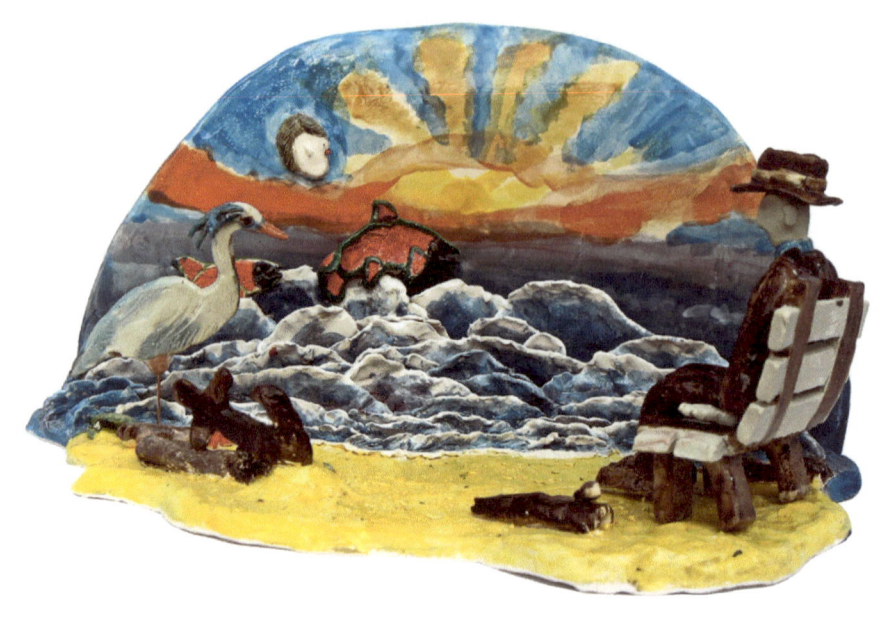

WHEN I'M OLD AND LONELY
Janet Magdanz

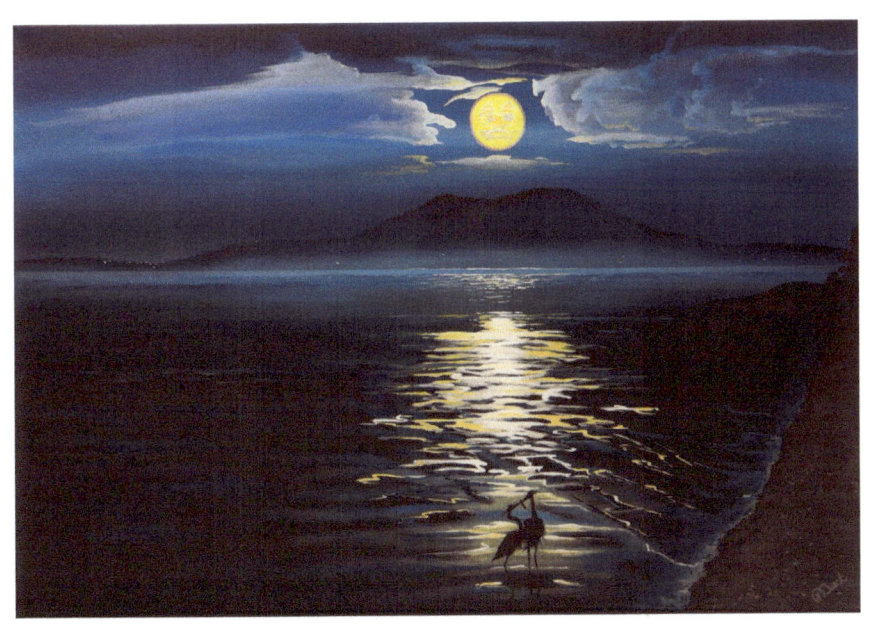

WHEN I'M OLD AND LONELY
Pauline Dueck

SNOW ON TIGGER

Cat eyes widen
Startled,
paws bat
as first flakes
graze his pink nose.

Whiskers twitch, shoulders hunch
and tabby fur quivers
when snow-cold rivulets
melt to his skin.

A dash, a squirm
through late autumn leaves, sere and brown,
half-body twist, spin to pounce
tail arcs with a swish.

Clouds part. Sunshine
vanquishes the intruders: intrepid first flakes.
Cat-genes recall eons of majesty: cat gods,
patrols in temple halls-
rectifies his demeanour, strolls home.

Mary Nelson

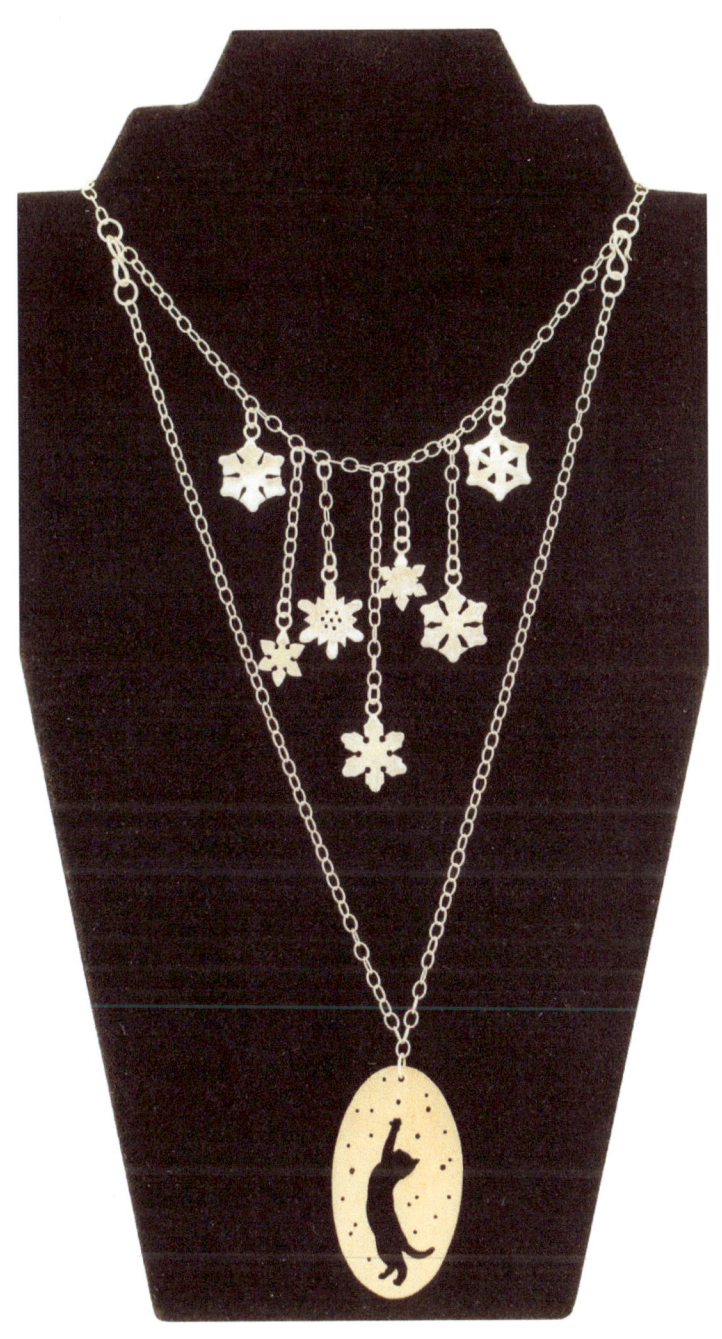

TIGGER IN THE SNOW
Susan J. Whyte

49

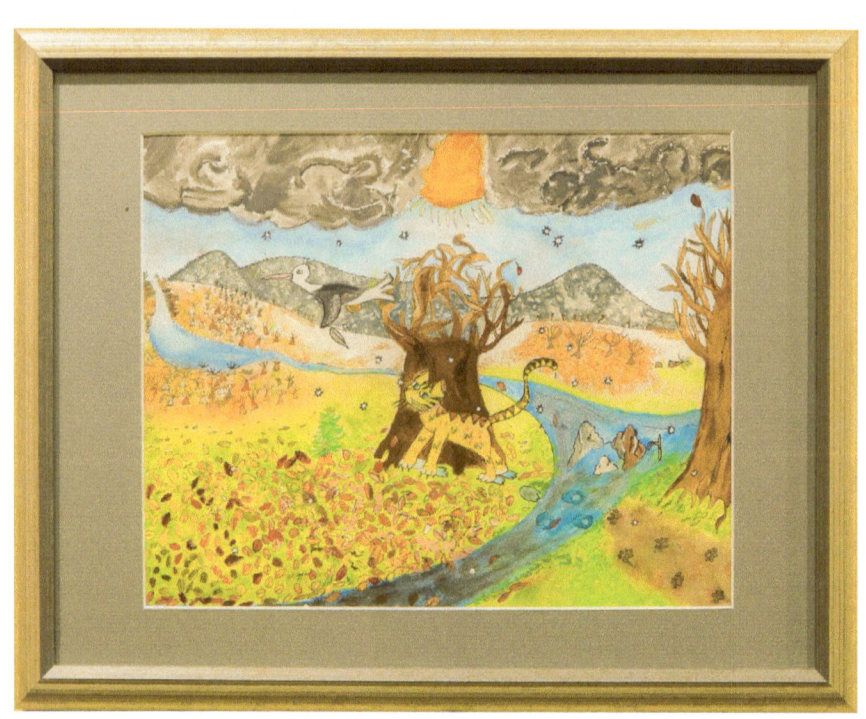

SNOW ON TIGGER
Naona Yamamoto

STRING OF BEADS (A True Story)

TERROR! STARK TERROR! Tiny Bobby awoke screaming and crying with tears welling from his eyes. Bobby's mommy lifted Bobby out of his crib and held him tenderly, making comforting noises, until Bobby fell into a snuffling sleep.

TERROR! STARK TERROR! Little Bobby awoke screaming and crying with tears welling from his eyes. Bobby's mother sat on the side of Bobby's bed and embraced him tenderly, murmuring comforting words. "Was it that nightmare again?" she asked. Bobby nodded "yes". "What is it like? What do you see?" Bobby whispered, "A string of beads, floating in the air." It didn't sound very scary.

TERROR! STARK TERROR! Bob could feel the fear starting to build in his sleep and wondered what it was about this nightmare that was so scary for him. He looked objectively at the nightmare and could see the string of beads floating in space, but there was nothing scary about the beads. It was the space, the vast, limitless space that was awesomely frightening. It wasn't threatening to him, but it was scarily overwhelming.

The lucid nightmare kept recurring unpredictably for many years, until Robert saw a movie which showed people dressed in white space suits venturing from their spaceship into outer space. From a distance, the people, tethered together, looked like a string of beads, floating in the vast, limitless space. After he saw that movie, the nightmare never came back.

The recurring nightmare conditioned Robert to look objectively and curiously at strange and potentially frightening events in his life. This openness and receptivity enabled him to enjoy many exceptional experiences: exchanging feelings, thoughts, pictures and influences with people, animals, plants and even insects, without the use of his physical senses and without being limited by differences in space and time.

He developed a consciousness of oneness with everybody and with everything in the universe, and indescribable feelings of peace, happiness and fulfillment.

Are these experiences and feelings available to all who are open and receptive?

Robert Radford

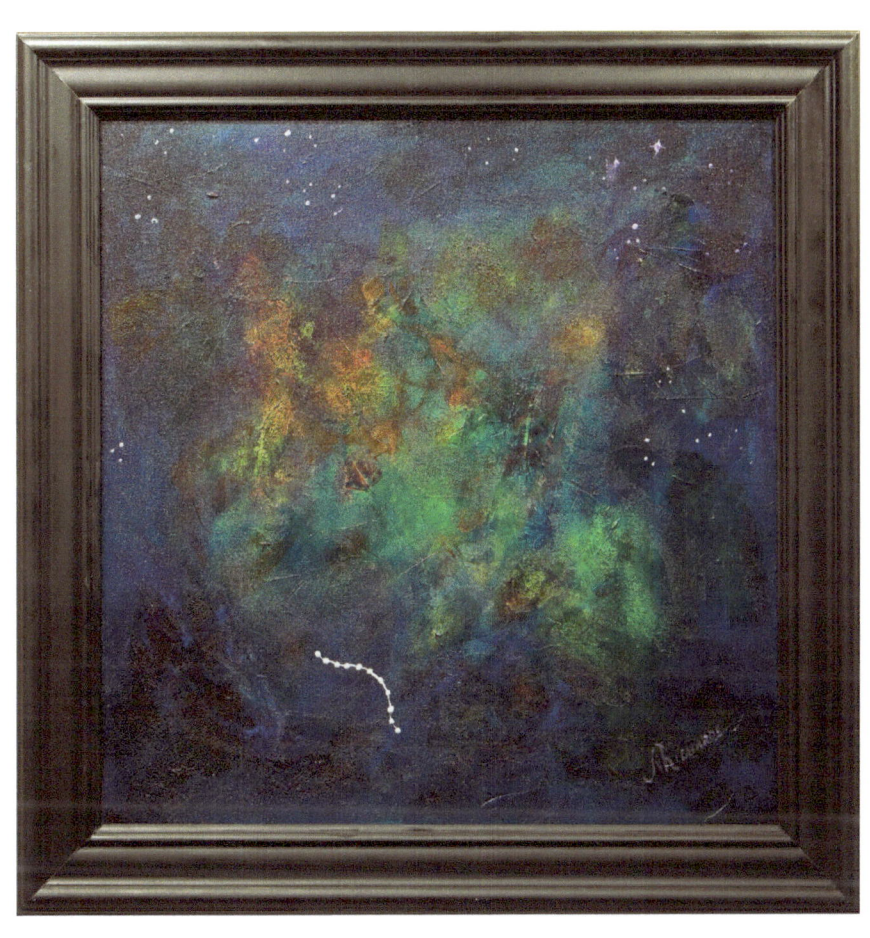

A STRING OF PEARLS
Arlie Richards

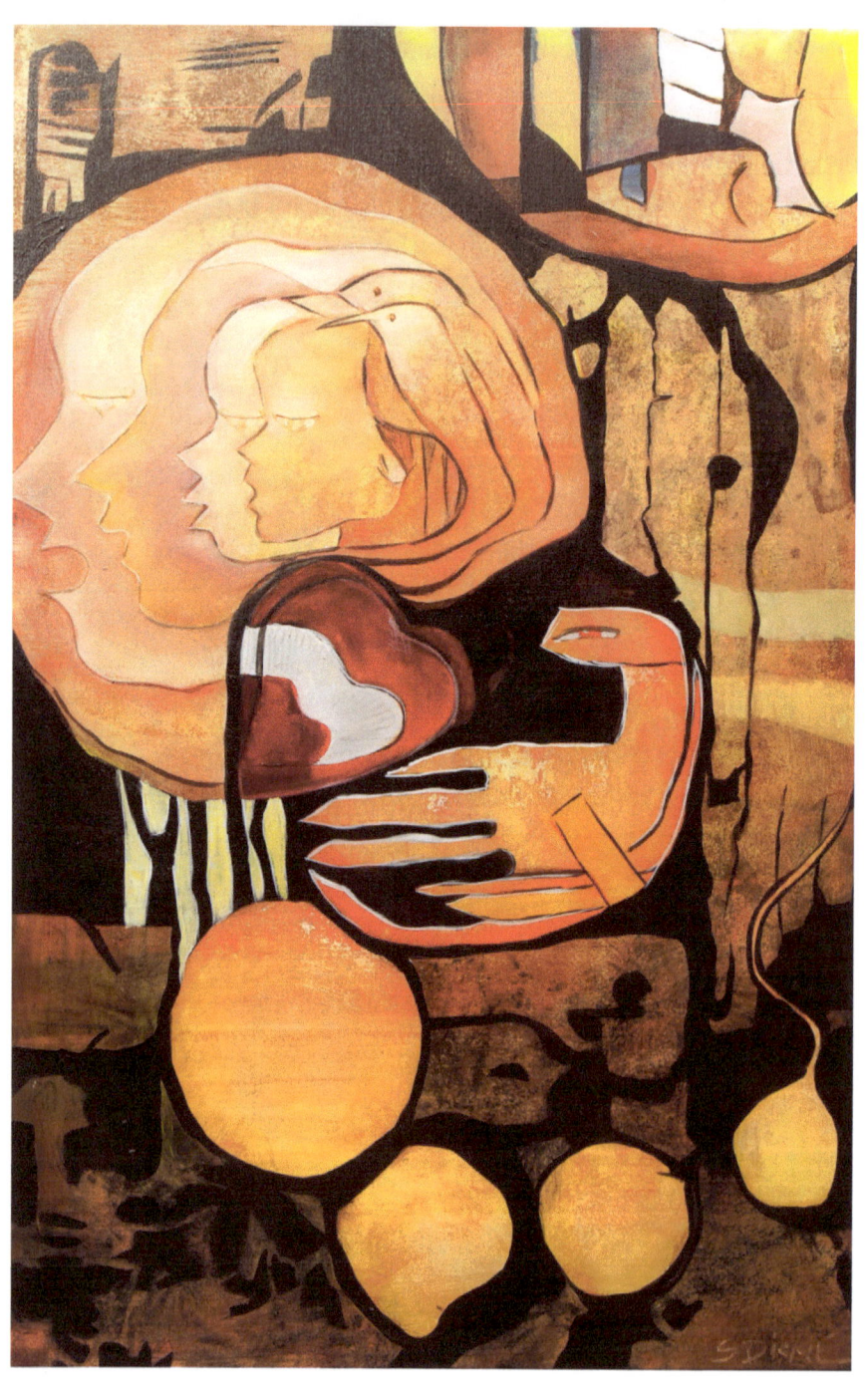

DARKNESS REVEALED
Shirley Dickie

FOG WALK

Chilled cheeks, crisp air
Sky water like cold steam
Gently pricks my skin.
This liquid air needs no umbrella
Yet all the trees and leaves are dripping
(Kinda like my nose).

Mossy twigs with silver teardrops
Precipitously hanging there,
Like shiny baubles, almost falling
(I admire the depths of those).

Silent landscapes, blanched and muted,
Enveloped grey unearthly forms
Like grieving spirits weeping round me
Soaking moisture into my clothes.

Thick with wetness, I can grasp
And touch, almost, the atmosphere.
Winter wraps its arms around me
(Now I'll go home and warm my toes).

Gail Robb

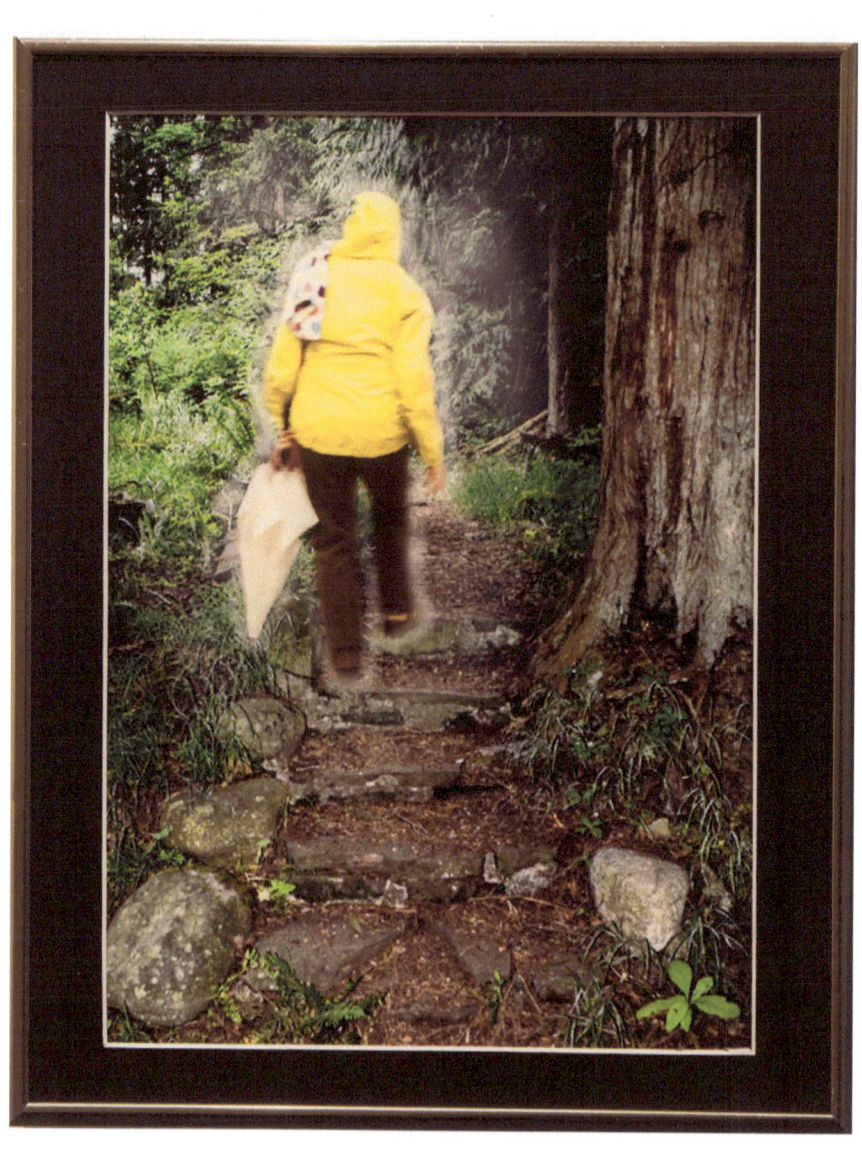

WALKING IN A FOG
Trish Rankin

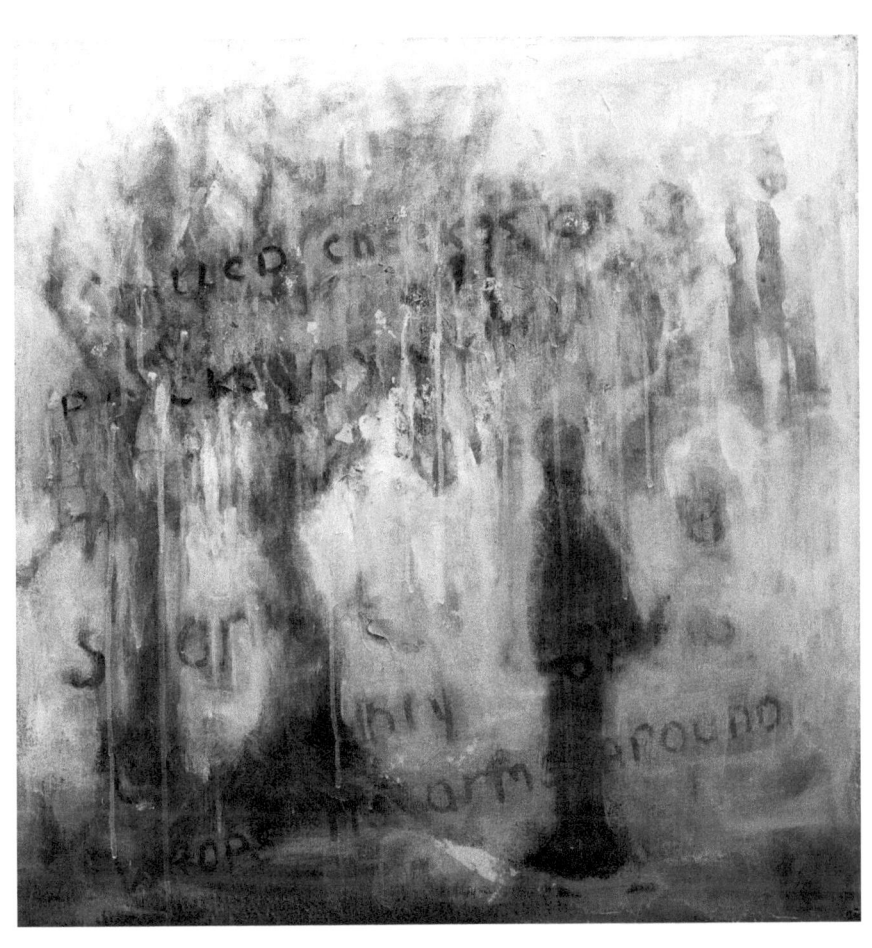

FOG WALK
Wendy Bradshaw

BERMUDA TRIANGLE

The maiden trip for this cruise ship would cut a swath across
The infamous haunt of 'The Mist', where boats and planes were lost.
Intrepid crew and skeptics who booked on felt well-prepared.
Technology – that was the key to safety, they declared.

Third day at sea, six heavily armed boats converged on them.
No place to run, greatly outgunned, the ship a floating gem.
They called for help – a pointless yelp, then wrote a final log.
And that was when the trapped captain perceived the sudden fog.

"The ship is doomed," the first mate boomed. "If we go through that
    mist."
The captain thought, *it's all we've got,* and gave the wheel a twist.
He told the crew, "They won't pursue, if we go straight in there.
I'd rather face what's in that place than a piracy nightmare."

The viscous cloud became a shroud, their gadgets useless now.
Said first mate to a nearby crewman, "I can't see the bow."
And then a 'door', a portal for the ship expanded wide.
They plowed on through the misty goo, and found themselves beside

A clipper ship that made the trip two hundred years before.
It bobbed beside a ketch now tied to smaller boats galore.
And further on they spied long-gone airplanes on land and sea.
Ashore were homes and fancy domes, lush fields and forestry.

"Choose any berth," a voice with mirth bellowed in a bullhorn.
"Then tell your tale, let us regale you, for we're all home-torn."
At last they knew what the Bermuda Triangle endows:
Beyond the mists, time coexists, and shares a single 'now'.

Gail P. Robertson

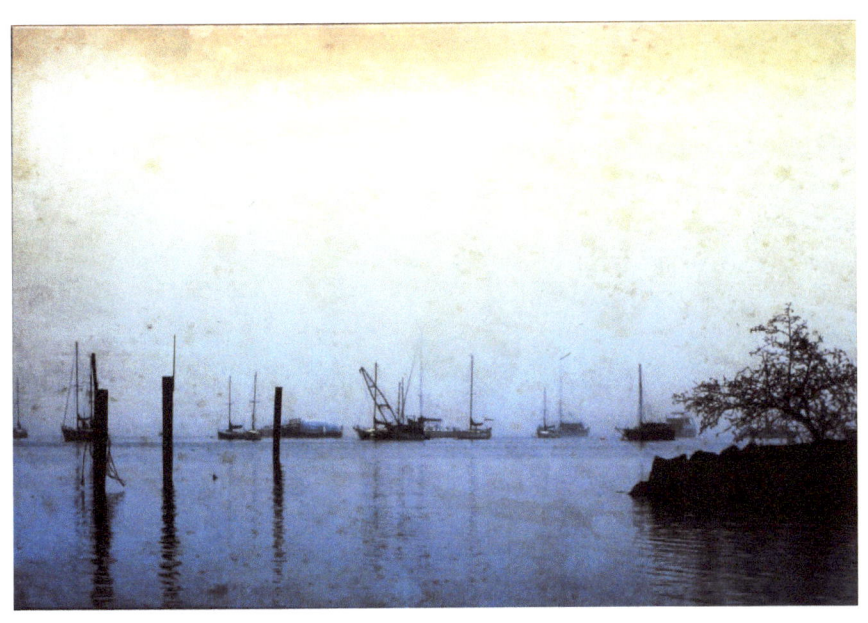

RESTING PLACE
Brigette Furlonger

MOVING INTO BLUE MYSTERY

the Gardener has left open the gates
unlatching sky's blue doors hung
singing high out over the sea's rhythm;
the Gardener has left
her shovel hooked to the lattice
its steely edge curves light
slicing afternoon's breastbone
open behind the heart day's loneliness
breathes:
wings poised in blue enchantment . . .

a Musician enters the abandoned gates
shakuhatchi knotted to his heart's sinews
he kneels at the water basin's edge
hears silence dropping on stone;
the Musician unknots his pipe
lays its wooden mouth to the watery membrane
breathes:
a shimmer of notes
floats from a chamber of ancient stone
a glimmering form
moon-painted face and lips a red-petalled peony
neck-stem curving crystalline
under ice shards and leafmold
trailing belly and thighs and high
between the breasts
a red slash
bares Her exquisitely winged
breastbone
. . .

Wendy Robison

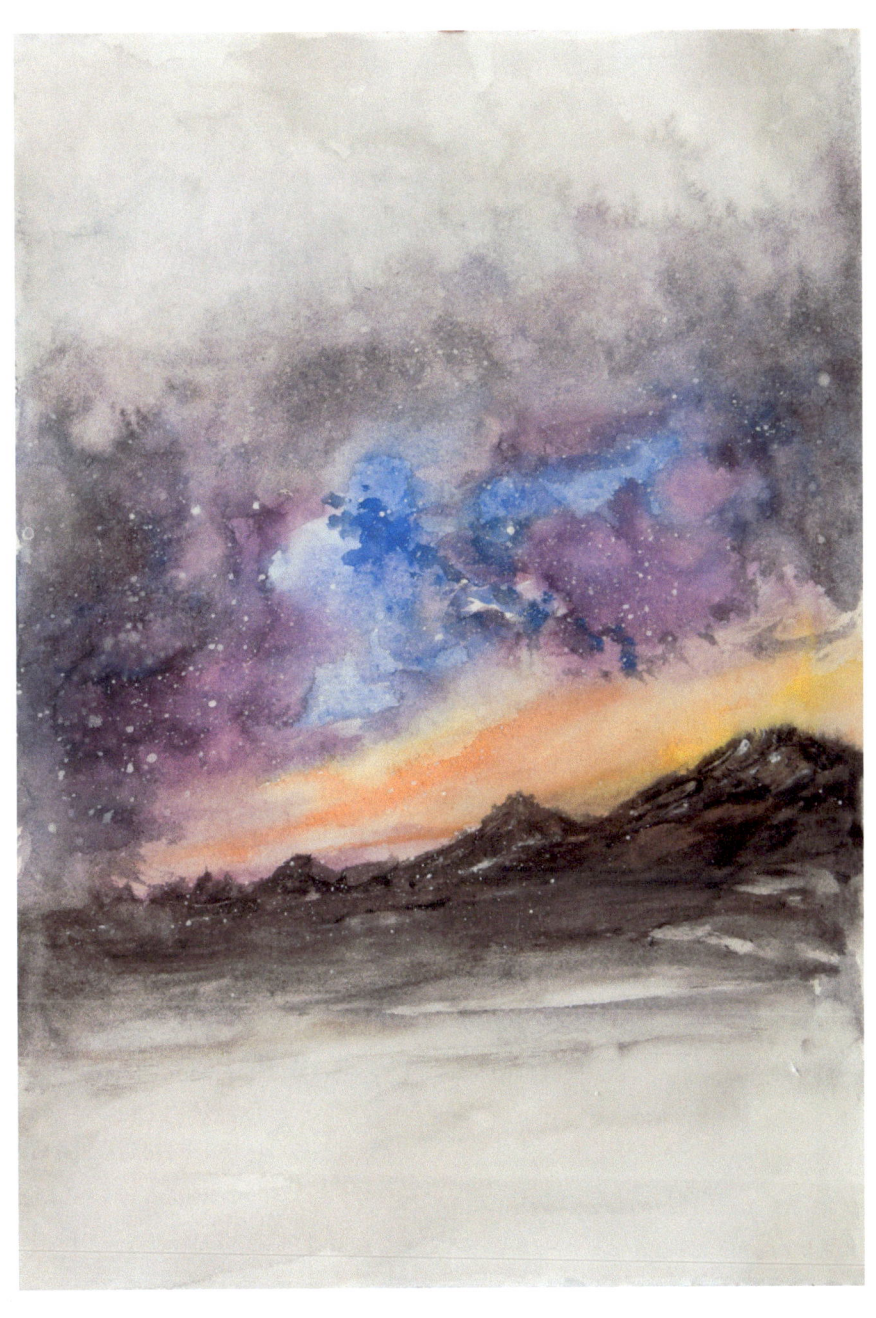

MOVING INTO BLUE MYSTERY
Angela Pistrucci

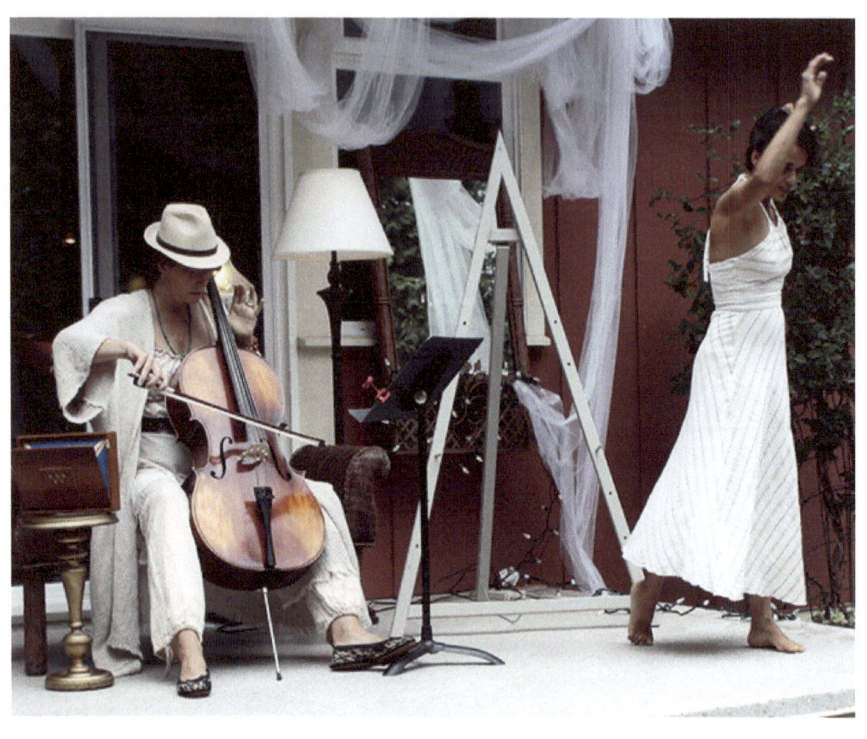

MOVING INTO BLUE MYSTERY
Musician: Cari Burdett
Creative movement: Marisa Jackson

MUSIC

(Dedicated to my friend Shoko Inoue, consummate concert pianist of renown)

Acoustic penetration: portals of the mind
Music: universal language,
Synesthesia colours imagination's palette,
Transporting every listener
Through vortices of emotion:
Harmony, dissonance to discordance
Ascends to heights of rapture or
Plumbs deep wells of sadness!

If granted the genome
Composers and musicians,
Translate thought to aural pleasure.
Molded vivid images pitch perfectly beheld
Transcend global boundaries
No culture, creed nor language,
Barricade such universal sound.
Encompassing humanity; one purpose one mind
Elixir of pain or pleasure no one declined!

Bruce Sand

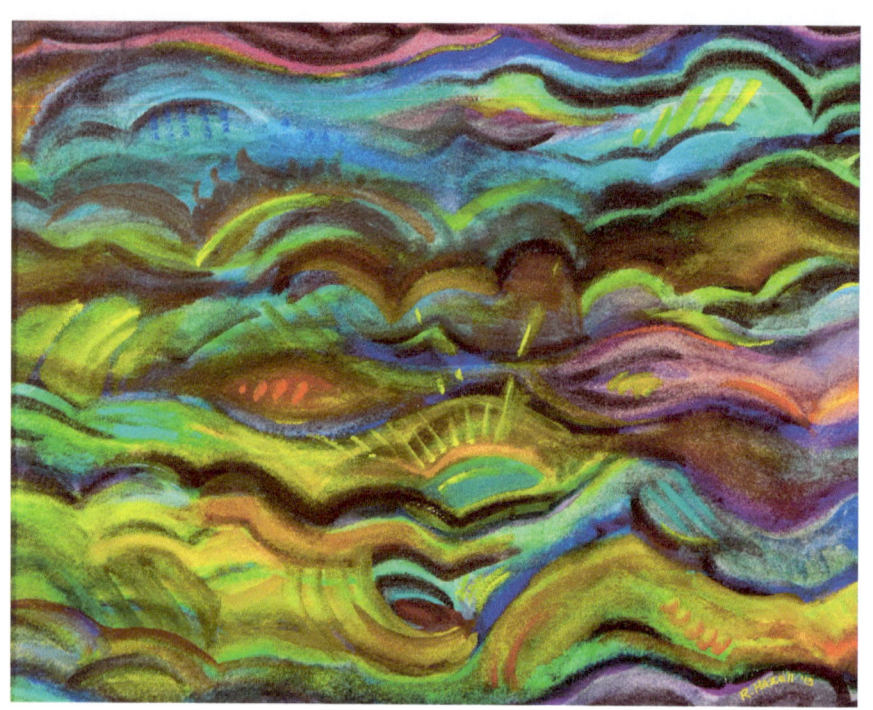

CODA
Rebecca Hazell

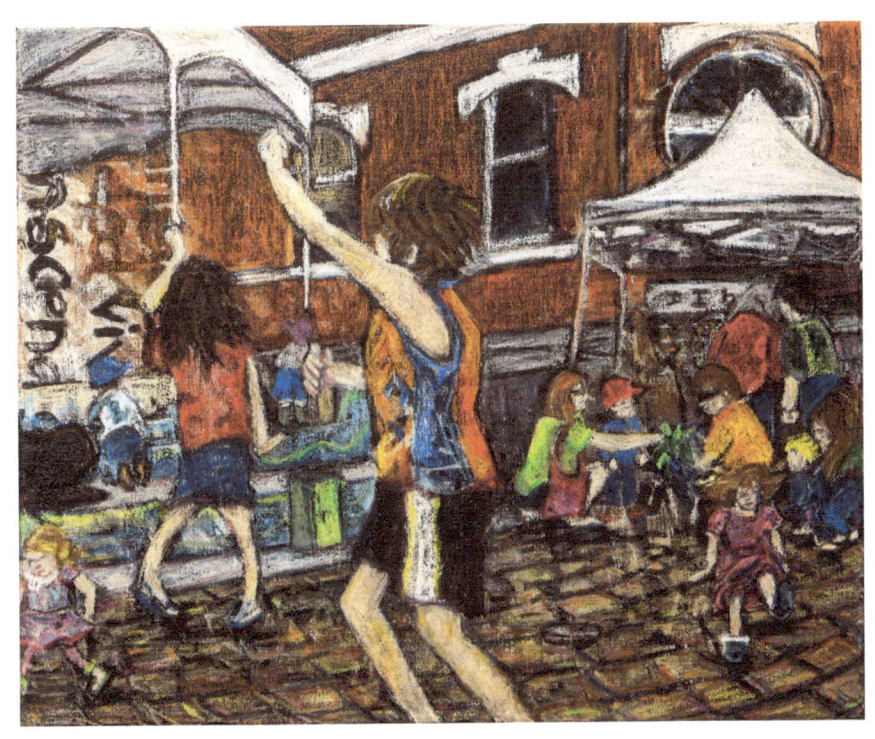

RESPONSE TO MUSIC
Ali Myhr

SHROUDED

The mist swirls leaving a blank, white world.
I step forward, wary lest I fall.
A sudden break – the ocean unforgiving,
the rocks ragged, slimy beneath my feet.
Landmarks blur shrouded with wisps of mist.
Then the world is white again.

I move with caution, senses confused, hesitate, and
stop.
There are no boundaries or guidelines.

Slowly, blindly, knuckles white, breath shallow,
adrenalin rushes and I move.
Nerves tingle, muscles twitch, ready to respond.
There is nothing to fight, nothing I can fix.
Slowly, one breath, one step at a time;
fleeing is not an option.

Voices around me close or far?
A dog barks.
The fog breaks, sun shines on a bright, defined world.
With confidence, I move forward.

Pat Scanlan

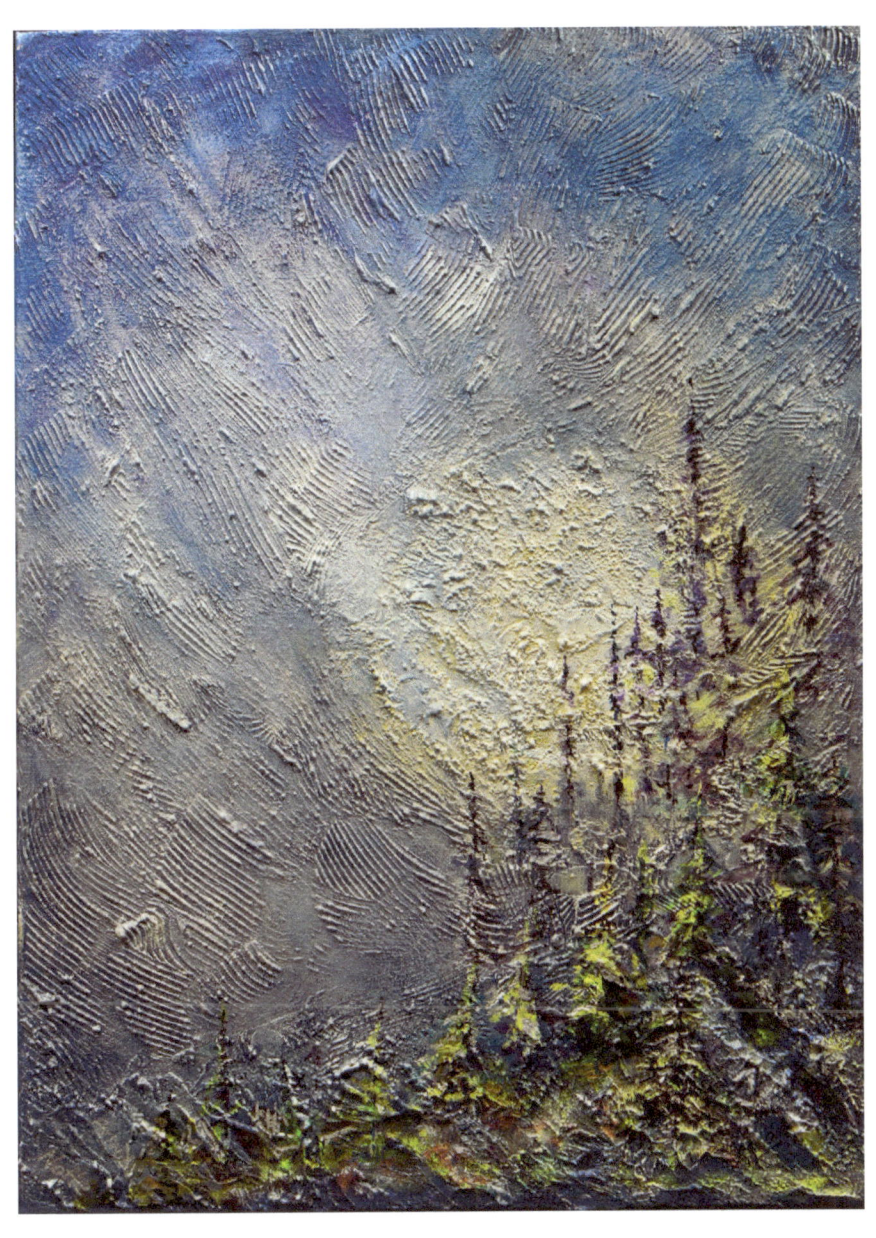

SHROUDED
Astrid Notte

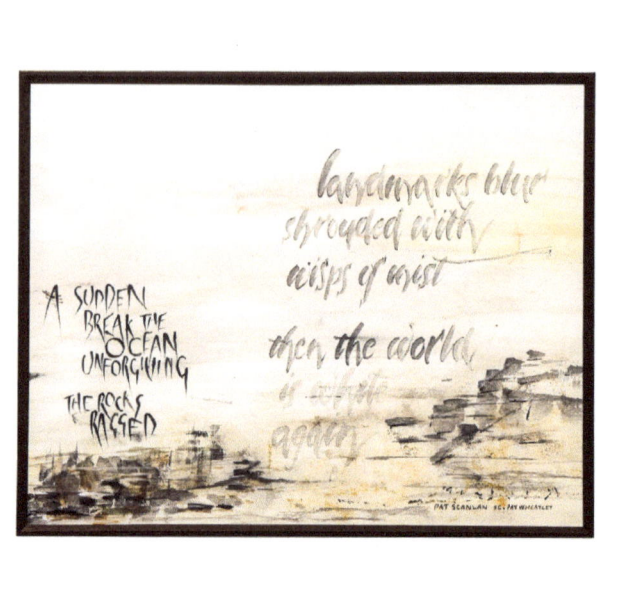

SHROUDED
Pat Wheatley

BEACH WALK, CHERRY POINT

Damp, firm sand
waves lap,
sighing faintly
as they wash the tide in.
Smell of iodine and brine.
Clouds fluff around the horizon.
Jake the dog runs
looking for seaweed to eat,
the kind with amber popping bladders.
Tiny red crabs scurry in from the waves
raising white pincers in the air
like combative, miniscule boxers.

More dog prints in the sand:
one set huge, the other tiny,
also a trail of deer hooves,
and, in a Robinson Crusoe moment,
prints of a bare human foot,
the toes dug in as if running.

Out in the bay a waiting freighter sleeps,
emitting a low hum over the water.
Apart from the hum
and the growl of a distant plane...
quiet.

Karen Severson

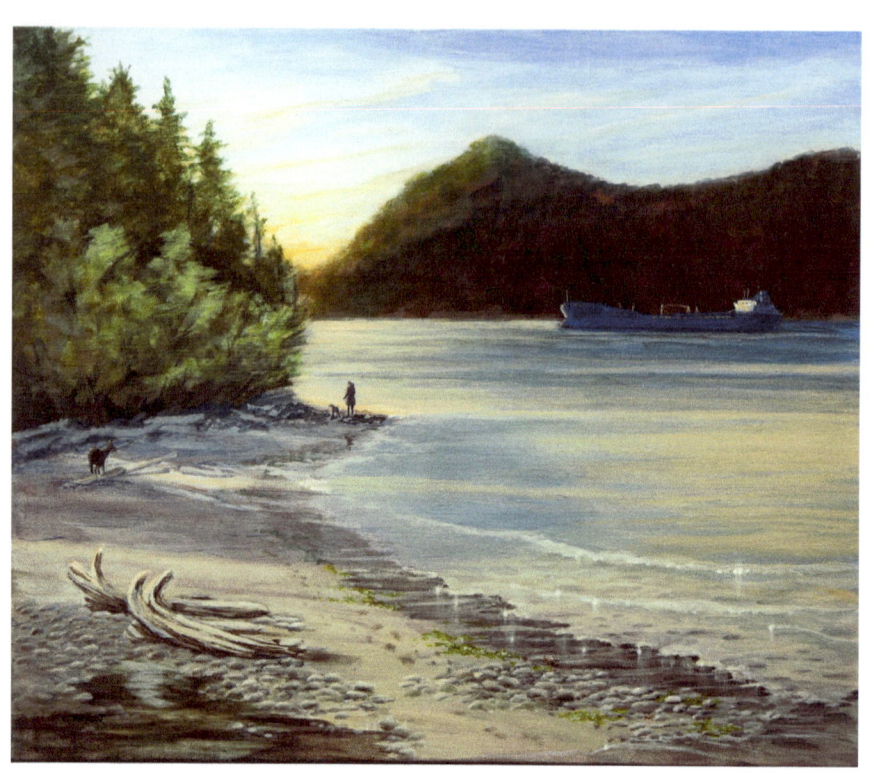

BEACH WALK, CHERRY POINT
Catherine Taron

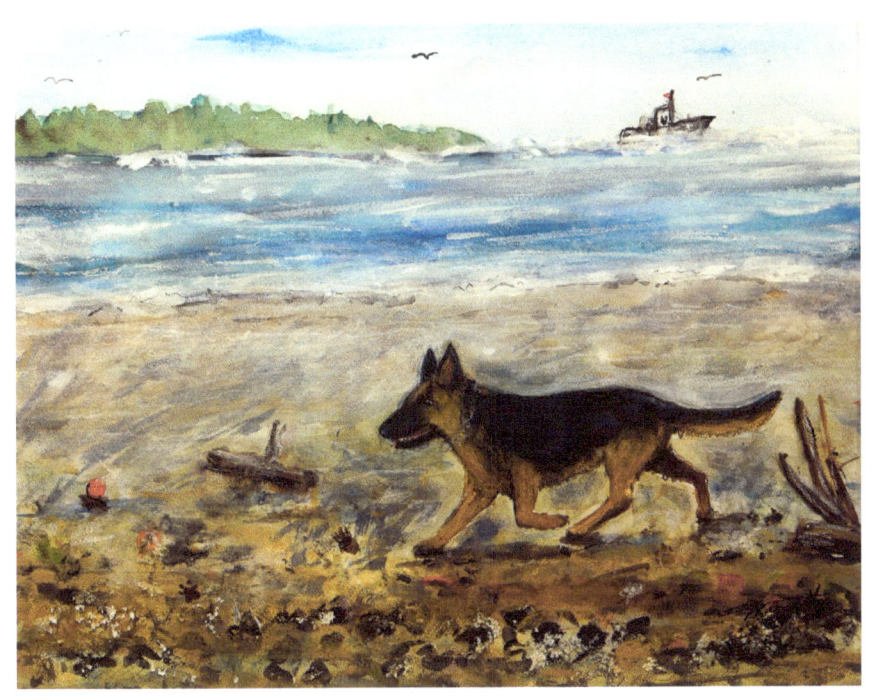

BEACH WALK
Margitta Ben-Oliel

OCTOBER COUNTRY EVENING

Through darkening fir and cedar green
air sweetened by seed sown, to rest
'til next Awakening

Sun, reclining, leaves long rays reaching far horizons
through the eye to warm a watcher's heart in
soft ruddy glow

English romantic pastorale - painter's dream: meadow and pond
country work a-field and husbanding
gentle labour bathed in dark warmth
in Earth and Sky embrace

While noble Clouds adrift upon vast heights
their Shining Glory amidst low'ring light lifts Spirit to soar …

In depths of nurturing fragrant body Earth
roots run deep, drink holy streams below …

And Moon, rise just past full
begins her journey from Eastern realms,
bathes our dark'ning world in warmth, her creamy radiance

Quiet songs of drowsing birds fade to almost silence, soft
evening air through forest ways

Retiring now from dampening evening
passing in, to warmth of hearth and company …

All rest in one another

John Mowat Steven

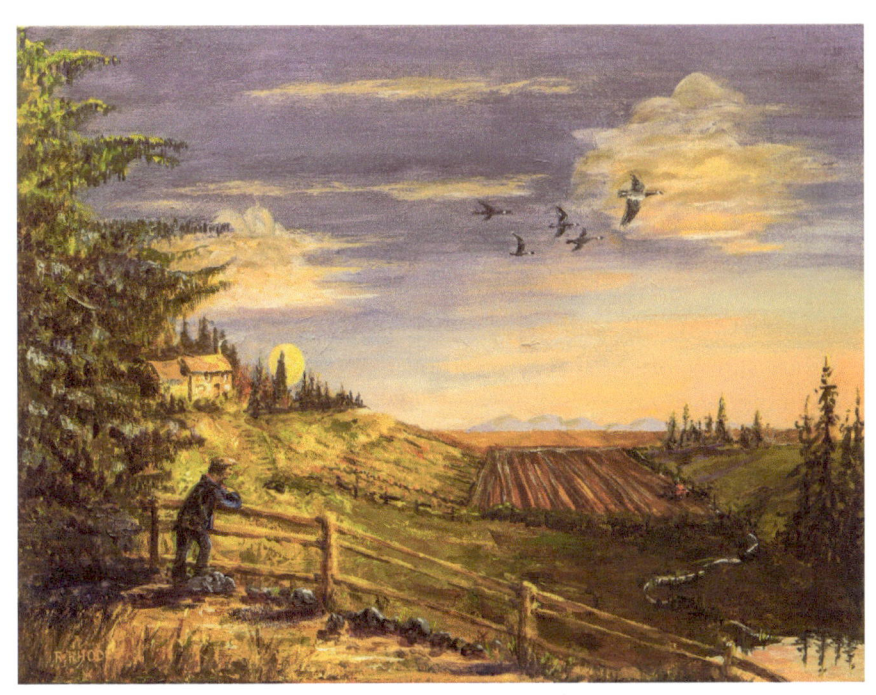

OCTOBER COUNTRY EVENING
Rae Rhodes

HER SEASONS

After the short cold dreary days of winter,
A wonderful change takes place.
Days lengthen and warm; the land turns green again,
Buds burst, blossoms open and Mother Earth begins anew.
>   SPRING
The rebirth of the seasons.

Days are sunny, bright and very warm;
Trees are now stunning with leaves that shade us.
Flowers vie for the sun to dazzle their colours
We once again experience Mother Earth in her glory.
>   SUMMER
The joyous season of growth.

As I walk down the country lane, I am aware of crispness in the air.
Flowers no longer abundant or their colours as powerful
Listen, you can hear a breeze, the scurrying of dry leaves fluttering to
the ground
Suddenly the air and Mother Earth are alive.
>   AUTUMN
The season of rest and renewal.

The days are short. The ground is now frozen.
Sun creates brilliant crystals on the newly fallen snow;
Evergreens covered in snow are majestic silent sentinels.
Shade trees stand starkly bare, their sap slowed to a crawl.
All growth is dormant. Mother Earth rests, she has come full circle.
>   WINTER
It's the end of the seasons.

Pauline Thompson

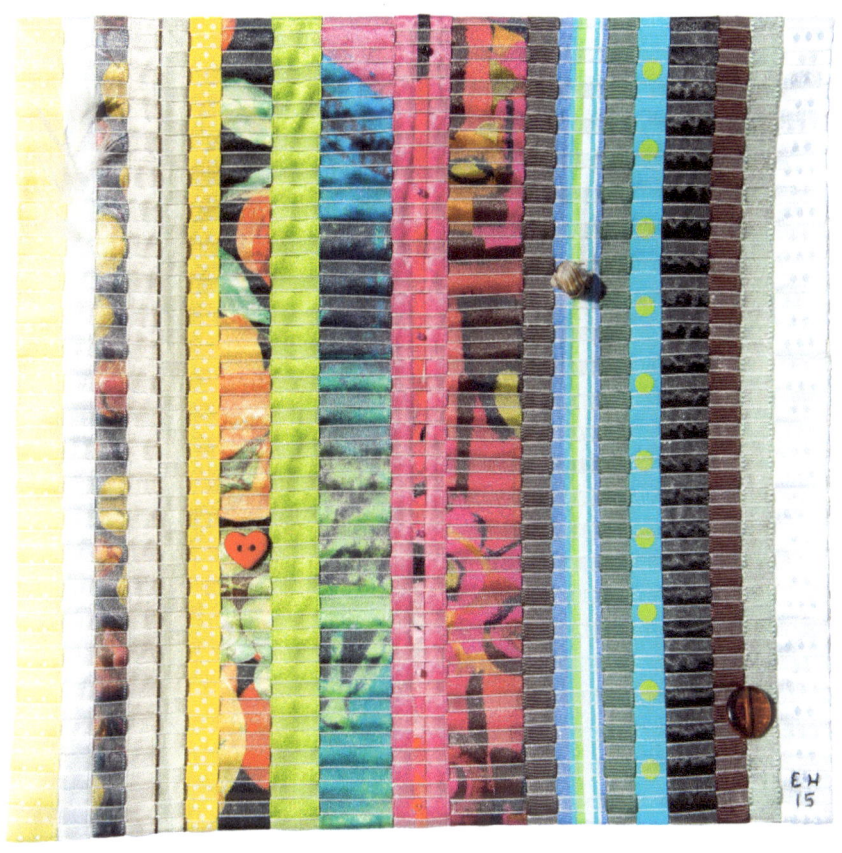

SEASONAL ABSTRACT
Ellie Hallman

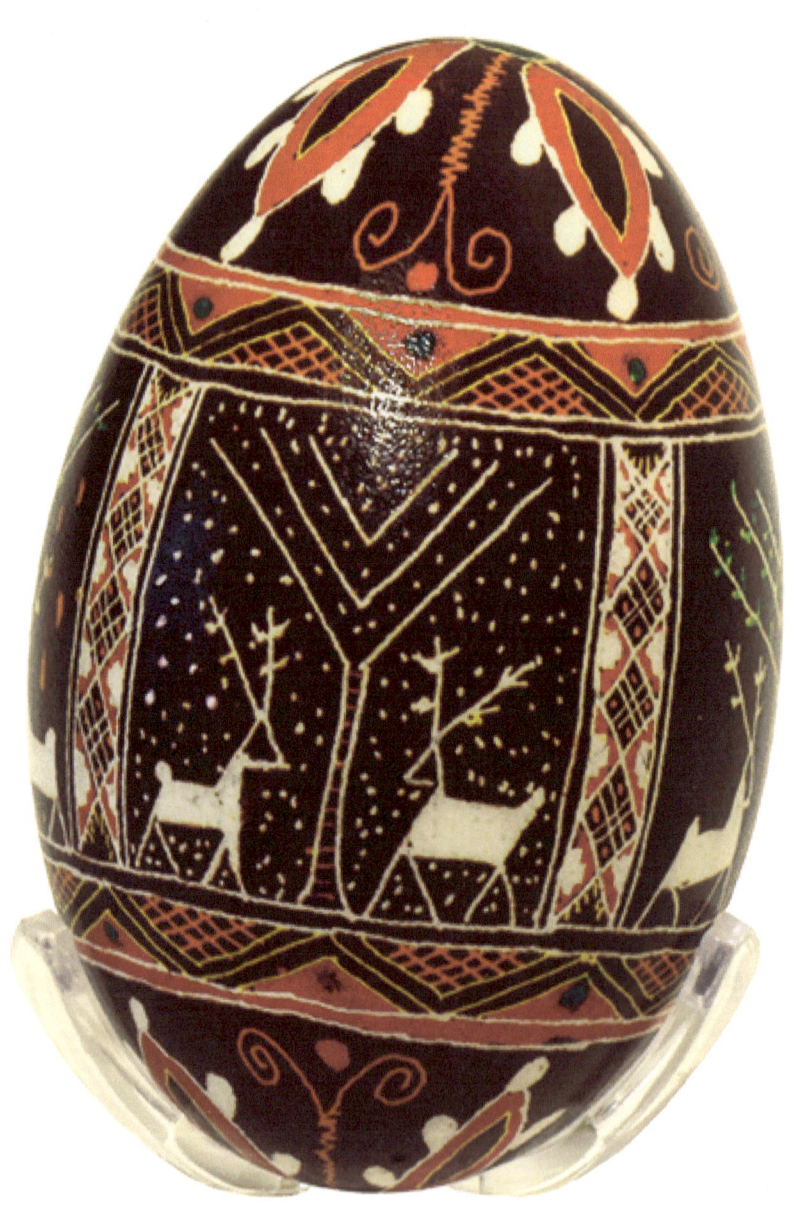

HER SEASONS
Pauline Thompson

SAILING ON OPEN WATERS

Open air against my face
Feeling the thrill of excitement rushing through my veins
Moving across open water with the sound of vibrating sails
And nothing else
How wonderful it is to harness Mother Nature's energy
To be in harmony rather than at odds
To be free to wander the open waters
To see the division between land and sea
To surrender one's safety to the call of the wild
Is to truly know what it means to be free
To cruise across mystery
An unknown world below that teams with life
The salty taste in the air reinforces my need for nourishment
Imagine how it would feel to live on open waters
The boundless opportunity to explore and not be tied
To any specific piece of land
To be able to connect with many different people and places
A whole new culture waiting to be uncovered

G. (Grant) Martin Waldman

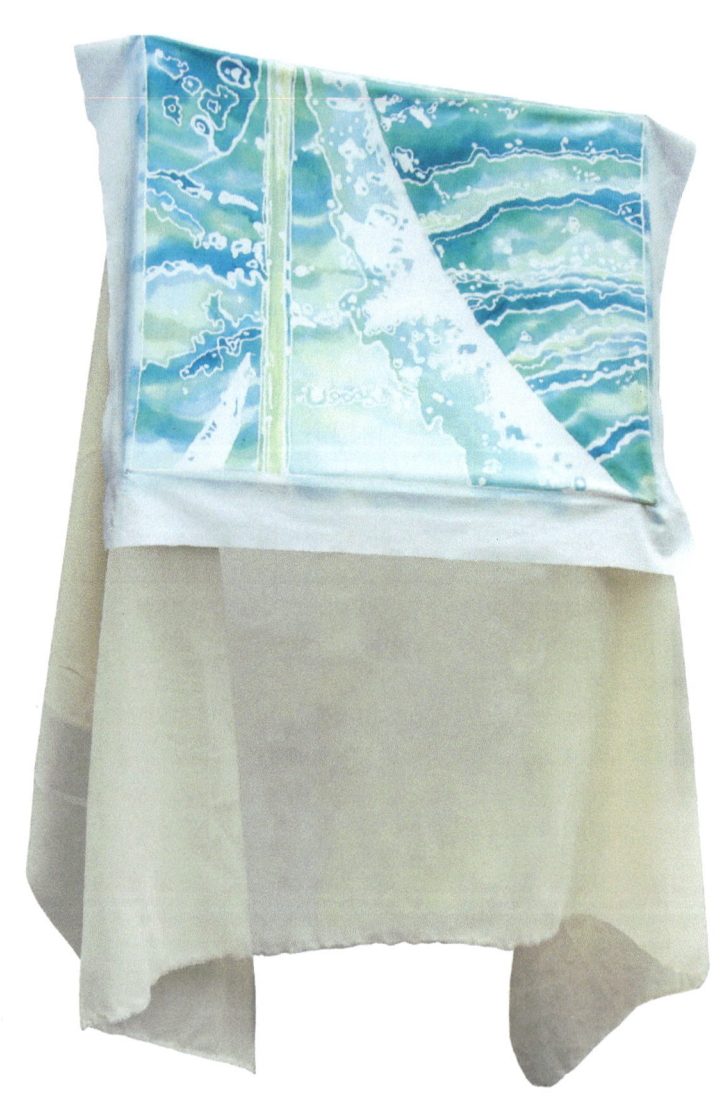

SAILING ON THE OPEN SEAS
Judy Brayden

MIGHT-HAVE-BEENS, ALMOST-THERES

I sing a song of frailty,
A drift of silent notes;
A spider's web of filigree;
A wraith I yearn to touch.

A skein of silken gossamer
Spread on a breath of air;
A sigh that's barely audible,
Never really there.

So small and insignificant
Some rights that make a wrong;
How meagre is a half tone
That slights a perfect song.

Nostalgic waves stalled on a nudge
Of sight, or smell or sound,
A haunting, yearning memory
Resisting being found.

When dreams have passed where
Do they go – they pale as fading light;
Subtle dawns and dusks of time,
Mere centuries in flight.

Reflective, transient tenderness
Bring sadness, longing, pleasure,
Frail strengths we own, forever ours,
Swathed gifts of life we treasure.

Pat Wheatley

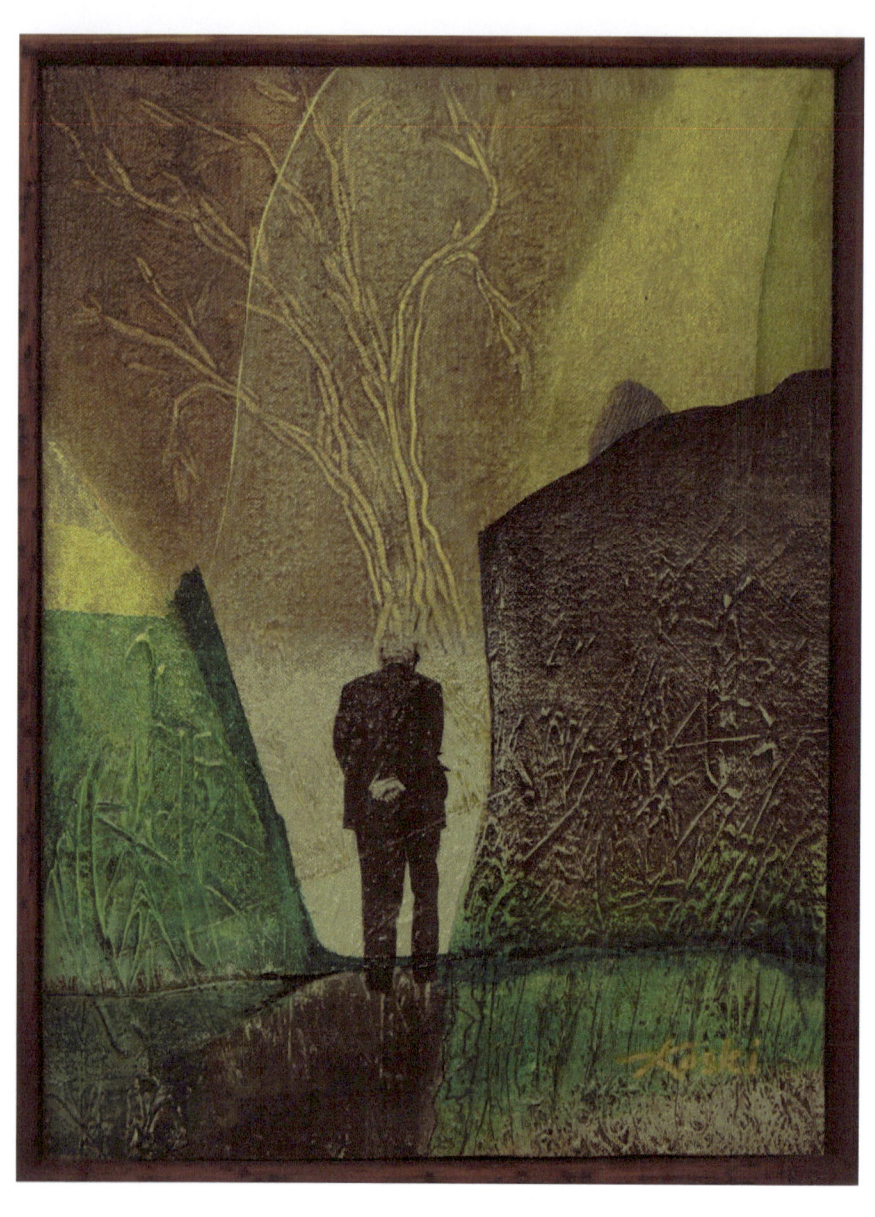

INTO THE FUTURE
Beverly Koski

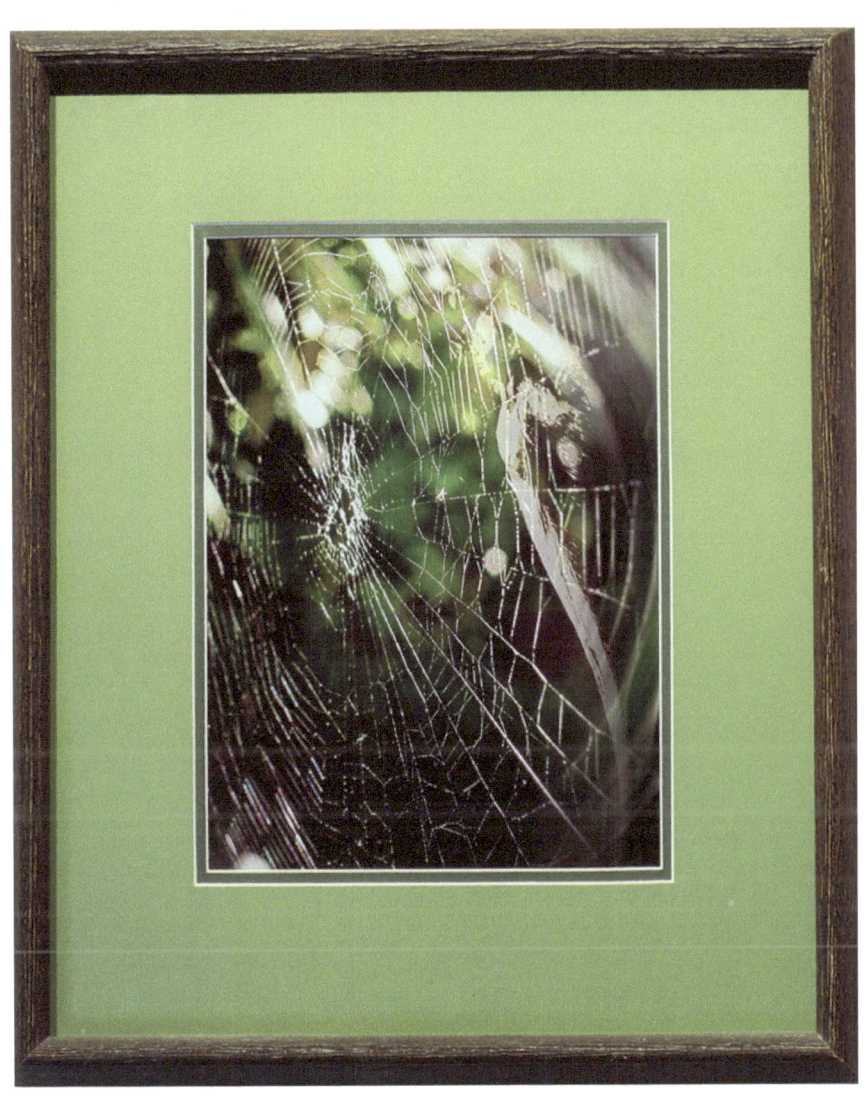

ALMOST THERES AND MIGHT HAVE BEENS
Frank Wall

QUESTIONS

What is it like to be so cold you can't feel your fingers or toes?
And what does a snowflake taste like when licked off the end of your
nose?

How do dry leaves of Autumn sound when crushed under trampling
feet?
What do you smell as they mount to the sky propelled by a bonfire's
heat?

What do you see on a warm Spring day when Autumn and Winter are
done?
These are the questions a child might ask whose seasons number but
one.

How sad that so many children in lands far away to the south
Have never shuffled through leaves of gold or felt icicles melt in their
mouth.

Linda Yaychuk

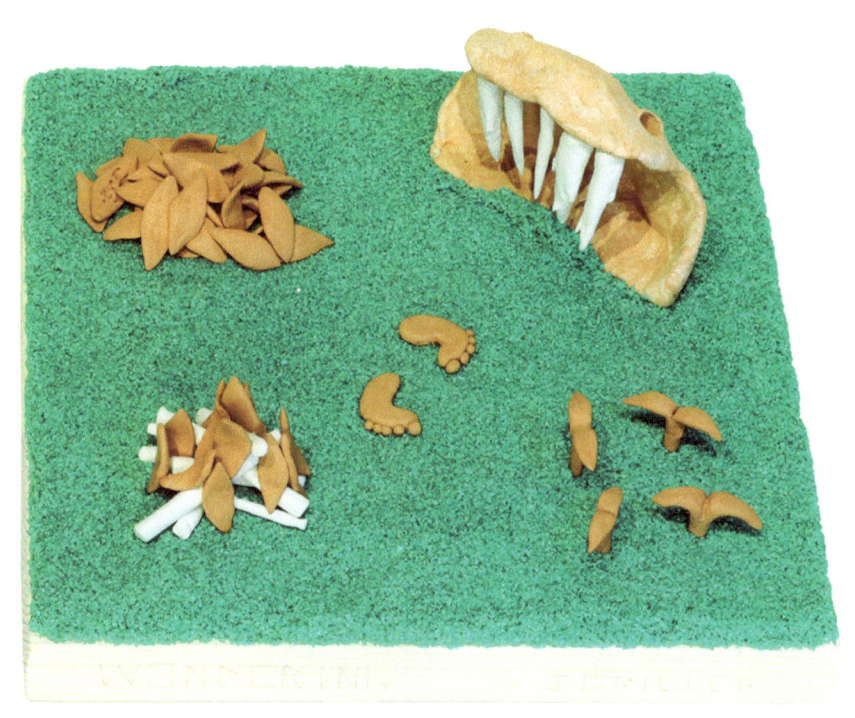

WONDERING
Jennifer Griller

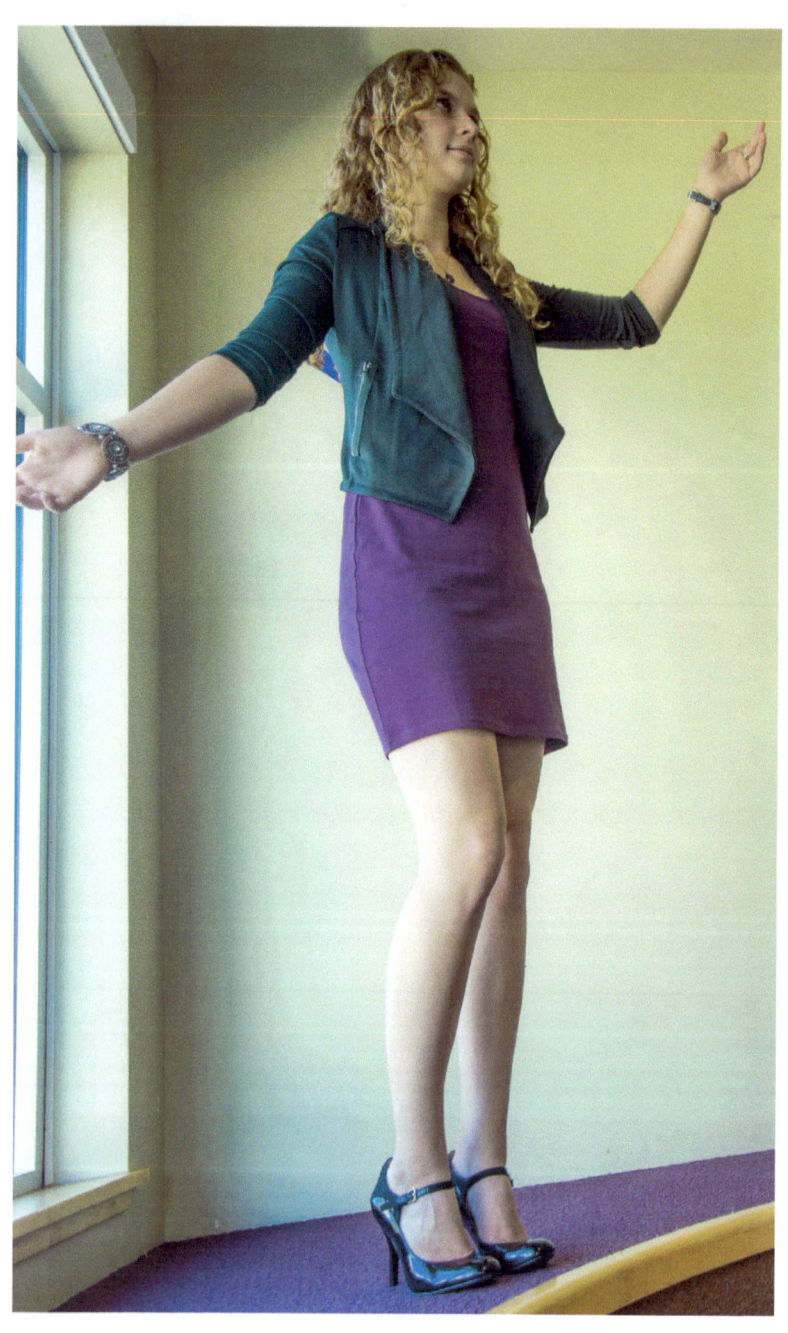

PLACE OF QUESTIONS
Creative Movement –
Samantha Furlonger

CAR

If I had a car I would take you
once in the front, maybe in the back,
over hill and dale, around corners
and curves, starting at your front door ...
so that fetching you, delivering you,
after going somewhere, and having you in
it driving together, four wheels going round,
one in my hands, a spare in the trunk, and
in the crack under my seat, findings: a lost
coin or hairpin or even a comb there with
the dust from pockets and winding gravel ...
we would return have driven through
space – where there are things to see, and
time – where there are things to do, having
traveled there where the ribbon of the road,
black and tapered, makes a point,
if I had a car.

Rojan Zét

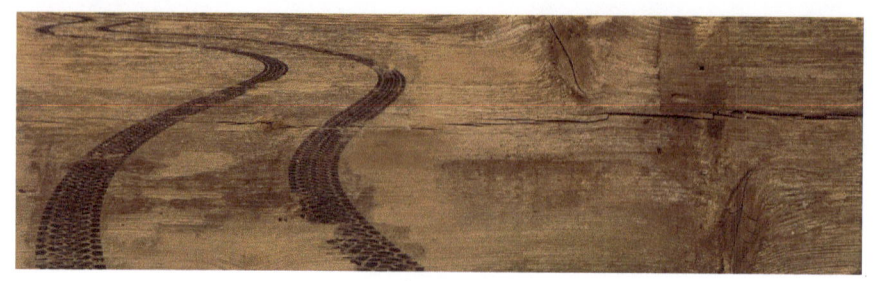

CAR
Sheila Le

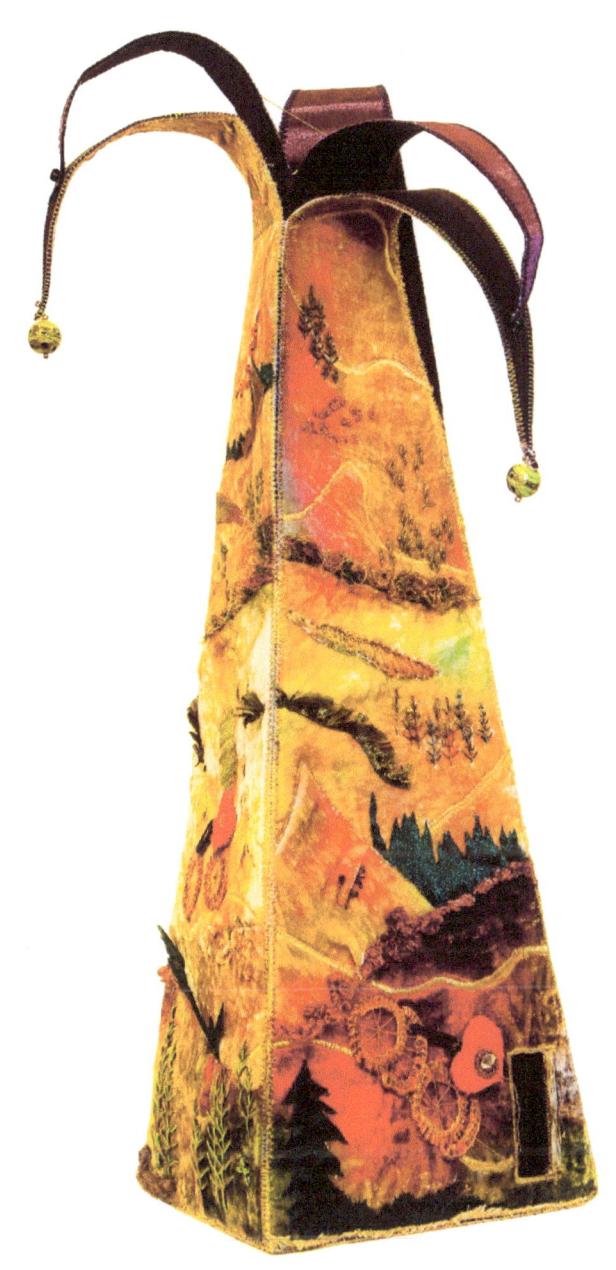

CAR
Gill Riordan